RAPHAEL NELSON

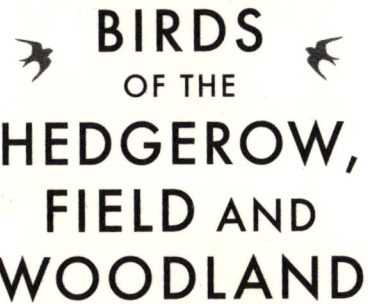

BIRDS
OF THE
HEDGEROW,
FIELD AND
WOODLAND

RAPHAEL NELSON

BIRDS
OF THE
HEDGEROW,
FIELD AND
WOODLAND

ILLUSTRATIONS BY THE AUTHOR

Unicorn Press Ltd

For Bernard Rorke; this token of a long and enduring friendship.

Unicorn Press would like to thank the Society of Wood Engravers and the
Royal Society of Arts for their help in trying to trace the author. In spite
of everyone's best endeavours we have been unable to do so.

Unicorn Press Ltd
66 Charlotte Street
London
W1T 4QE

www.unicornpress.org

10 9 8 7 6 5 4 3 2

First published in 1943
Published by Unicorn Press Ltd 2014

ISBN 978-19100-65242

Cover designed by Felicity Price-Smith
Printed in India by Imprint Digital.

• AUTHOR'S NOTE •

I N SPRINGTIME, from hedgerow, field and woodland comes a chorus of rich and varied bird-song. The music of our native Song Thrush, Blackbird and Skylark is joined by that of the Nightingale and Blackcap, who cross the seas to spend the summer with us. It is the season of Nature's musical festival.

But bird-song is only one of the many facets of wild bird-life. To see and recognize the birds of the countryside in their natural haunts, and to know something of their lives and habits, is to bring a fuller richness to our appreciation, our enjoyment and interest.

It is my hope that those who have hitherto felt little urge to explore the world of birds, as well as bird-lovers and students of natural history, will share with me here some of the pleasure it has given me to produce these descriptive pieces and illustrations of many of the birds which haunt our fields, woodlands and waterways.

• CONTENTS •

Missel Thrush	8	Great Titmouse	54
Song Thrush	10	Blue Titmouse	56
Redwing	12	Long-tailed Titmouse	58
Fieldfare	14	Coal Titmouse	60
Blackbird	16	Marsh Titmouse	62
Ring Ousel	18	Crested Titmouse	64
Stonechat	20	Golden-crested Wren	66
Redstart	22	Wren	68
Robin	24	Kingfisher	70
Nightingale	26	Dipper	72
Blackcap	28	Bearded Titmouse	74
Greater Whitethroat	30	Pied Flycatcher	76
Lesser Whitethroat	32	Spotted Flycatcher	78
Garden Warbler	34	Pied Wagtail	80
Dartford Warbler	36	Grey Wagtail	82
Chiff-chaff	38	Yellow Wagtail	84
Willow Warbler	40	Blue-headed Wagtail	86
Wood Warbler	42	Tree Pipit	88
Reed Warbler	44	Meadow Pipit	90
Marsh Warbler	46	Red-backed Shrike	92
Sedge Warbler	48	Skylark	94
Grasshopper Warbler	50	Woodlark	96
Hedge Accentor	52	Swallow	98

• CONTENTS •

Swift	100	House Sparrow	142
House Martin	102	Tree Sparrow	144
Sand Martin	104	Corn Bunting	146
Nightjar	106	Yellow Bunting	148
Green Woodpecker	108	Cirl Bunting	150
Great Spotted		Reed Bunting	152
Woodpecker	110	Snow Bunting	154
Lesser Spotted		Starling	156
Woodpecker	112	Carrion Crow	158
Wryneck	114	Rook	160
Tree Creeper	116	Jackdaw	162
Nuthatch	118	Magpie	164
Cuckoo	120	Jay	166
Chaffinch	122	Kestrel	168
Greenfinch	124	Sparrow Hawk	170
Hawfinch	126	Tawny Owl	172
Bullfinch	128	Barn Owl	174
Goldfinch	130	Long-eared Owl	176
Brambling	132	Short-eared Owl	178
Linnet	134	Little Owl	180
Lesser Redpoll	136	Wood Pigeon	182
Siskin	138	Stock Dove	184
Crossbill	140	Turtle Dove	186

THE MISSEL THRUSH

AS WELL as being the largest of his tribe – he has a length of 28 cm – the Missel Thrush is paler than the other thrushes, his plumage being of a grey, ashy tinge.

A favourite habit of this attractive bird is to perch in the topmost branches of a lofty tree, and from there to pour out his song for all the world to hear. Even when the weather is squally and wet he will continue to sing, as though in defiance of the driving rain and blustering wind. For this reason he is also known as the Stormcock.

For the greater part of the year the Missel Thrush keeps to the woods and to open spaces of the countryside. But on the approach of spring he leaves his wilder haunts to set up a home and rear a family. Having chosen his mate the pair start the search for a nesting site. Fruit trees in orchards and gardens are great favourites for this purpose, in a fork of which the nest will be built.

The main materials used are mud and twigs for the frame, hay and grasses for the lining. Up to five light blue-green eggs with mauve-brown markings are laid during February, March and April.

Most of the Missel Thrushes I've seen foraging for food were busy hauling up fat earth-worms, but the bird also takes many insects and will readily devour a snail. In the winter he lives mainly off berries of various kinds, including those of the mistletoe, which gives him his name.

The Missel Thrush is with us all the year round and is well spread throughout the British Isles.

THE SONG THRUSH

ALTHOUGH the countryside is his natural haunt, gardens are equally good places in which to watch the ways of the Song Thrush, who shows little fear of man. I've often stood no more than a yard off as a thrush tugged a struggling worm from its hole, and neatly nipped it into several pieces before feeding them to its nestlings. It is interesting, too, to observe him extract snails from their shells. These he dashes with force against a large stone until the shell is smashed. The bird is a bold robber of soft fruits in season, but against this he devours large numbers of insect pests. His winter fare is mainly the wild berry.

If the winter is mild, nesting will start as early as February. By the second week in April nests are usually complete with first clutches. The chosen site is generally in a hedge or tree, though very odd and unlikely places are sometimes selected. Rarely are they more than a few feet off the ground. In shape the nest is like a small cup, into which the sitting bird fits snugly. The shell is made chiefly from coarse grasses and is lined with mud. The five eggs laid are an attractive light blue spotted in black at the wider end.

The olive-brown plumage, white throat and speckled breast of the Song Thrush are as familiar as his delightful warbling notes. He measures about 23 cm in length. He is to be met with all over the British Isles.

Throstle is another name by which this bird is widely known.

THE REDWING

AS AUTUMN approaches many birds leave us for warmer places abroad, and in compensation a large number wing in from across the sea to spend the winter here. Among these winter visitors are the Redwing and Fieldfare, two handsome members of the thrush family. First to arrive is the Redwing, small groups of them soon showing up about the countryside.

It is because the Redwing is almost as large as the Song-thrush and resembles him in other respects, that it is easy to confuse the two. Nevertheless the rich red-brown sides and the light strip above the eye of the Redwing make him quite distinctive to the observant watcher.

The Redwing usually feeds off worms, snails and a wide variety of insects; but should the weather turn severe and cause his ground food to become scarce, he will depend on wild berries to stave off hunger. A hard winter affects him too, in that he is less robust than our resident thrushes, and often succumbs to an icy snap. During such spells of weather large numbers of Redwings die off.

It is quite a common sight to see fairly large flocks of these birds in the fields, where they often become prey to the Sparrow Hawk. They roost together for safety in dense undergrowth or in coarse grasses.

From naturalists who have studied the bird in his Northern breeding haunts we know something of its nesting habits. The materials used for the nest, which is sited either in a bush or tree not very high from the ground, are chiefly twigs and grasses. Up to six eggs of a green tone, carrying markings of red-brown, are laid. Usually two families are reared. The bird is considered by many to possess a pleasing singing voice.

THE FIELDFARE

FROM A little way off the Fieldfare looks like a deeper-toned Missel Thrush, but a closer inspection of him will reveal that his colouring is a merging of slate blues and warm browns. His head, neck and rump are a slate blue, his topcoat a rufous tint; his throat and breast are tawny-gold. He is next in size to the Missel Thrush, measuring 25.5 cm in length.

Instances have been reported in the past of the arrival of the Fieldfare in this country by the end of September, but this is exceptional as they do not ordinarily arrive until October is well advanced. Like Redwings, they cross our coasts in large flocks, at times in the company of Redwings and our native thrushes.

The long journey from the Fieldfare's Northern breeding haunts leaves the bird famished and weak, and on arrival his first thought is of food. Hips and haws are the berries he favours, but he also picks up what he can from the open fields where, if the weather is not too hard, he is often to be seen. But, as in the case of the Redwing, a bitter spell of winter weather often proves too much for him, and many weaken and die.

A few stragglers sometimes stay until May, but most have left before April is out. They return to their breeding grounds in the forest belts of Scandinavia and Russia. Here, in a nest generally placed in the fork of a fir or bush, up to seven pale blue eggs, with red-brown markings, are laid during May.

This handsome Thrush, which has a local name of Bluebird, is widely distributed about the British Isles during his stay here.

THE BLACKBIRD

THE BLACKBIRD is the sentinel of the hedgerow. At the first sign of danger, he fills the air with his shrill scolding note of alarm to betray the approach of the intruder, be he fox or man. But the bird also has a singing voice of infinite purity which he uses to charm us with his fluty song.

The silky black cloak and yellow bill of the male Blackbird are known to most people, but the female is less readily recognized. She is dressed rather drably in a sober brown, and her dull buffish breast carries markings resembling those of the Song Thrush. But no thrush has the hen Blackbird's length of tail. The full length of the adult Blackbird is 25.5 cm.

Hedgerows and shrubs are the common nesting-places of the Blackbird, but his liking for setting up home in a bush in the garden helps one to get to know something of his ways at first hand. Nesting begins early, and a brood before March is out is by no means uncommon. The nest itself is made from bents and grasses with a sprinkling of mud at the base. There is a lining of less coarse grass. The eggs are a pretty green-blue and are well mottled with red-brown. Up to six are laid. At least two families are reared.

Earthworms, which are fed to the nestlings, are the chief food of the Blackbird, but many kinds of insects are devoured in large quantities. Snails, too, are taken. His winter fare is for the most part the wild berry.

There are few areas in these islands where the Blackbird is not to be seen.

THE RING OUSEL

I F IT were not that the Ring Ousel carries a crescent-shaped splash of white about the throat he might well pass as a Blackbird. He is, in fact, known locally as the Moor Blackbird, which gives a clue to the nature of the locality in which he spends the summer with us. The hen bird also has the crescent-shaped gorget about the throat, but it is much duller in tone, and the rest of her mantle lacks the richness of her mate's. The Ring Ousel is slightly larger than the Blackbird, having a length of 28 cm.

An early visitor, the bird is sometimes with us before March is out. His dominion is the wild and solitary moor or heath, flanked by mountain or hill. Occasionally he will forsake these lonely wastes to visit outlying farms in search of fresh fruit or other titbits.

Worms and insects are his usual food and, later in the year, berries.

Rough and desolate country such as the Ring Ousel haunts offers a wide choice of sites for a nest. A dense patch of heather, a hole in a bank or a rock-crevice, are the favoured nesting-places. Up to five eggs, green-blue like the Blackbird's, but more richly marked, are laid towards the end of April. In shape and materials used the nest is very much like the Blackbird's. Threats to the safety of eggs or nestlings are faced by the parent birds with great courage and boldness.

The song-notes of the Ring Ousel are poor compared to the Blackbird's.

The bird usually leaves us during the autumn. While here he keeps chiefly to moorland haunts in England, Wales and Scotland.

THE STONECHAT

TO HAVE a good chance of observing this attractive little bird it is necessary to make for a furze common. There the Stonechat may often be seen sitting on a spray-tip in clear view, though he doesn't give you much time to study him before he is off again. His colourful coat rarely fails to catch the eye; black head and white collar are offset by a rich chestnut-red breast. The female is less warmly plumaged. The length of the Stonechat, who is a resident bird, is about 14 cm.

Towards the end of April, sometimes earlier, the nest is begun. The materials chiefly used are grasses and moss for the framework, and a lining of hair, fine bents and feathers. Great care is taken to conceal the site of the nest, which is usually placed in the depths of a furze bush. A clutch of up to six eggs is laid. These have a ground tone of pale blue-green, faintly spotted, with red at the wider end. Some have been found without markings. More than one family is reared. When nesting is over the bird is inclined to rove.

When foraging for food the Stonechat has the Flycatcher's and Wagtail's habit of hawking insects on the wing. Nevertheless his staple diet is taken from the ground in the form of worms, seeds and similar fare.

The song of the Stonechat is soon over, but it is pleasant to the ear while it lasts.

Of the many local names he has earned for himself, that of a Stonechatter would seem to fit him best with the sound of his oft-heard alarm note, which strongly resembles the jingling together of two pebbles.

This delightful little bird is no stranger to the heaths and commons of these islands.

THE REDSTART

THE ARRIVAL of the Redstart, who is usually here by the first half of April, is looked forward to by many bird-lovers, for he is a frequent and welcome visitor to our gardens. But it is not only in gardens and their vicinity that we find him; a liking for solitude takes him sometimes to moorland districts far removed from cultivation and the haunts of man. Yet, wherever he may be met with, his dapper and colourful appearance will not fail to attract attention and earn our admiration.

His black throat and dark slate-blue topcoat are just the colours to emphasize the contrast of his rich rust-red breast and tail. The tail, which has given him the local name of Firetail, is particularly noticeable, especially when caught in the sun. He is 13.5 cm long.

The Redstart has the Robin's habit of choosing odd places in which to set up his home, his nest sometimes being found in the beams of outhouses and sheds, and sometimes in flower-pots or other receptacles left about the garden or orchard. But his more normal choice is a tree-hole. In those areas where old stone walls abound a ready-made crevice will be used. The six eggs, usually laid during May, are a light blue, sometimes tinged with green. Roots and moss chiefly form the walls of the nest, which is lined with hair and wool or feathers.

Almost every kind of grub and insect is eaten.

The Redstart pipes a brief but tuneful note.

Although he may be seen in the north of England he seems to favour the Southern Counties. He leaves us sometime during September.

THE ROBIN

THE ROBIN REDBREAST is one of the most fearless and perky of all British birds. It would almost seem that he seeks out human society, and more than once I have coaxed one to take a crumb of bread from my hand. Once in Devonshire, a few years ago, while I was sketching from a bank of the River Dart, a Robin alighted on my shoulder, stayed long enough to glance at my work, and then flitted off to a nearby branch as though none too pleased with what he had seen !

The Redbreast's coat is too well-known to need description by me, and the same is almost true of the many places he chooses in which to nest. These may range from an old watering-can to an empty flower-pot, but a more common site is a hedgerow-bottom or beneath an old tree-stump. Sometimes the bank of a stream will be selected. The materials used are usually leaves and moss, which receive a lining of hair.

Up to six eggs of creamy-white, splashed with either light-brown or red markings, are laid between the end of March and beginning of April. By nature the Robin is courageous and often quarrelsome. Any other of his kind who enters what he considers to be his private domain does so at his peril, for he will drive the intruder off with furious attacks. The Robin has a clear, flute-like, warbling song. His diet is mostly worms and insects, fresh fruit when he can get it from gardens and orchards, and those scraps he can pick up from his many human admirers.

He is about 14.5 cm in length.

THE NIGHTINGALE

THE NIGHTINGALE, whose exquisite singing is extolled in verse and legend, has no striking plumage to catch the eye. Like most of the songbirds he is quietly arrayed and can boast no brighter tones than a chestnut-brown above, and a drab white below. His mate is more soberly clad. The Nightingale has a length of about 15 cm.

You are more likely to hear the delightful song of this bird than to see him. For the most part he is a shy and retiring creature who sets up his home in the depths of a furze bush, usually in the vicinity of oak trees. Oaks seem to hold a big attraction for him. Well-screened from the outside world, the paired birds begin to gather in the materials for their nest early in May. Dead oak leaves comprise the material, though those from other trees are also used. To the leaves are added a little grass to form the shell, and into this goes a lining of roots and down. Generally the eggs, of which up to six are laid, are an olive-brown, though sometimes they may vary to a dull blue-green.

Worms and insects are the main food of the Nightingale, but he varies this diet with fruit and such berries as he can find.

It is the male bird which arrives here first, usually about the middle of April. Earliest to leave are the young, generally in August, the parents following in September.

The Nightingale is more common in the South than elsewhere in these islands.

THE BLACKCAP

FEW OF our bird visitors are more welcome than the Blackcap, who reaches us by the second week in April. His rich black crown is the one strong colour-note of his plumage, the rest of it being broken into tints of ash-grey and ash-brown. The brightest patch of his undercoat is his white belly. But although the Blackcap lacks colour in his plumage, he more than makes up for it by his mellow, lilting song, so often to be heard in the hedgerows during spring and summer. He has a length of just under 15 cm.

The fondness of the Blackcap for currants and raspberries is, perhaps, the reason why he sometimes chooses to nest in orchards and gardens, although the more customary nesting-places are in hedgerows and thick bushes. In these, generally not very high off the ground, he sites his nest. Bents and roots form the framework to a lining of hair. The eggs, of which up to five are laid early in May, vary in colour : some have a dull-creamy ground, with brown-red blotches, others incline to a reddish base, with markings of the same colour. Two families are usually bred.

Although the Blackcap will help himself liberally to garden fruits, credit must be given him for the large amount of insect-life which he devours. Worms and grubs, beetles and weevils, are only a few of the pests he includes in his diet.

It is thought that a few of these birds stay the winter with us. Usually, though, they leave during September.

The bird is no stranger to most parts of the British Isles, but is less common in the North.

THE GREATER WHITETHROAT

OUR HEDGEROWS during spring and summer would be the poorer without the pipings and scoldings of the Greater Whitethroat, who comes to tenant them about the second half of April. He leaves again early in September. He is a cheerful bird who doesn't mind showing himself, especially during nesting-time, when he is busy finding food for his young, and warning intruders against coming too near his home. The habit of this bird of running mouselike about nettle-beds has earned him the local name of Nettlecreeper. He is 14 cm long.

The upper plumage of the Greater Whitethroat, with head and neck of ash-grey and a warm brown back, is pleasingly offset by the splash of white on chin and throat and the buffish breast with its faint rose tint. The hen bird is many shades duller.

Low down in a hedge or thicket, the Greater White-throat builds his nest. It has a deep, cosy well, which is made chiefly from fine grasses and receives a lining of hair and bents. The first clutch of six eggs is to be found in the nest towards the end of May. Some of them have a green-yellow base blotched and spotted in a mauve-grey, others carry markings of a light brown or grey-green.

Like the Blackcap the Greater Whitethroat is fond of fresh fruit, but is a less frequent visitor to our orchards and gardens. Mainly he feeds off insects of various kinds.

Of the large family of visiting warblers the Greater Whitethroat is probably the most widespread. He is to be heard and seen almost everywhere in these islands during his stay with us.

THE LESSER WHITETHROAT

THE LESSER WHITETHROAT gives you less chance to see him in his haunts than his cousin, the Greater White-throat. He is a much shyer bird, fewer in numbers, and is smaller in build. His song is not as pleasing as the Greater Whitethroat's; he is an interesting bird and well worth looking out for. He resorts more often to trees than the larger bird. Insects are his main food.

The two warblers look alike; but there are slight differences in plumage which help to distinguish between them. The Lesser Whitethroat's back isn't quite so warm a brown, and his belly carries a larger and whiter patch. His bill is darker. The hen bird is more dully garbed. The male bird is 13.5 cm in length.

A hedge of bramble or coarse undergrowth, where the bird is unlikely to be disturbed, are the sort of places the Lesser Whitethroat chooses in which to build his home and rear his family. The nest is not quite as careful a structure as his larger cousin's and is sometimes placed higher off the ground. It is more loosely put together, and is shallower. Grass and roots, with a lining of hair, are the main materials used. Up to six eggs, creamy-white in tone, and carrying markings of brown and ash-grey, are laid during May.

The Lesser Whitethroat arrives about the middle of April, but keeps to certain parts of the Midlands and Southern Counties. Wales knows him well, but in Scotland he is rarely seen. He leaves before September is out for his winter home in Africa.

Of the many local names by which the bird is known, that of White-breasted Warbler well describes his appearance.

THE GARDEN WARBLER

THIS FINE songster sometimes arrives before the end of April, but more often it is the beginning of May. He leaves in September. The best place in which to listen to his music and catch a glimpse of him is in a wood or coppice. Every now and then he will show himself from behind a curtain of leaves, but he is a wary and suspicious bird, and will instantly slip behind a leafy screen if he thinks his safety is endangered. The bird also visits gardens for what he can pick up in the way of fresh fruit.

Like other songsters the plumage of the Garden Warbler is a sober one. His topcoat is a uniform olive-brown, while below the general tone is a buff-tinged dull white. He has a length of about 14 cm.

A bush of bramble or thorn is the usual place chosen in which to rear a brood, but now and again a nest is set up in a dense shrub in a garden. It is neatly, but not too strongly, built from bents and roots, and is lined with hair. Up to five green-tinged, grey-white eggs, with mottlings of green-brown, are laid early in May.

The food of the Garden Warbler consists of insects of many kinds, to which are added fruits in season, especially currants and berries.

The bird tends to keep to Southern areas throughout England and is by no means common. As the range extends Northwards his numbers considerably decrease.

Greater Pettychaps is an old country name for this bird.

THE DARTFORD WARBLER

THE EXTREME shyness of some birds, who take great care to conceal themselves from human view, is often the reason why we consider them to be scarce. I think this can be said of the Dartford Warbler who, the moment he is disturbed, dives into the depths of a dense furze bush and is very reluctant to show himself again. A little patience, though, will reward the bird-watcher's efforts. Sooner or later the bird will leave his hide-out and settle himself on a spray-tip of furze, where a good view of him may be had. He is a long-tailed, short-winged bird, not difficult to recognize.

The spring is the best time to see something of his ways, for it is then that he flits from one clump of furze to another, stays for a brief second or two, then starts all over again.

The Dartford Warbler is not a colourful bird, but his slaty-brown topcoat and his undercoat of a purply-tinged chestnut, broken by an off-white belly-patch, are not un-pleasing. The bird is 13 cm in length.

The Dartford Warbler loves the furze heath or common, and it is usually in a thick clump of gorse that he places his nest. Bents and furze go to the making of the shell, which is lined with fine grasses and a small amount of hair. Up to six eggs, carrying brown markings on a green-white ground, are laid during April.

The bird is less common than he was once thought to be, and keeps to certain parts of the country. He is with us all the year round.

A popular local name is Furze Wren.

THE CHIFF-CHAFF

THE TRIM little Chiff-chaff often arrives in the British Isles before spring has had a chance to show something of its green freshness. It is one of the remarkable mysteries of migration that this feathered sprite of under 13 cm in length is able to make the great flight from his winter quarters in the Mediterranean to his nesting grounds in Britain. Although Chiff-chaffs have been known to arrive as early as the middle of February, they do not usually appear until the second week in March. Very soon after their arrival they get down to the serious business of mating and rearing a family, and it is at this time that the lively notes of their song are most in evidence.

The Chiff-chaff has a yellow-tinged, olive-green coat, and an undercoat of yellow-white. Both cock and hen are similarly garbed so that it is not always a simple matter to distinguish between them.

In the choice of nesting-site the Chiff-chaff has broad views. He will set up his home in a hedge, or among brambles ; in tall grasses or in a low thick bush. The nest itself is generally placed a little way off the ground. It is made from dried leaves, grass and moss, into which goes a lining of many feathers. It is domed in shape, with a hole near the top large enough to allow the parent birds to enter or leave at will. The eggs, of which six or more are laid during April, are spotted with either purple or dark-brown on a white base.

Insects are the Chiff-chaff's main food.

The bird is more numerous in the south than elsewhere in these islands. He leaves us in the autumn.

THE WILLOW WARBLER

THE CHOIR of woodland songsters is added to during the second week in April with the arrival of the Willow Warbler. He is also known as the Wood Wren. Although the bird haunts the woodlands, where he spends much of his time high up in the tree-tops, he is also to be seen in fairly open country provided that ready cover is at hand. He visits gardens, too. His sweet song is one of the delights of the countryside.

You may possibly catch a glimpse of him as he flits about a hedge or coppice, or when he comes to snatch some currants from the garden. He bears a marked resemblance to the Chiff-chaff, but his topcoat carries a tinge of stronger yellow and his legs are of a lighter shade. The Willow Warbler is slightly larger than the Chiff-chaff. Male and female are closely alike.

The Willow Warbler prefers to build his nest among thick, coarse grasses on the ground, but you might well come across one at the base of a bush or hedge or the tall tangly grasses of a bank. The nest is dome-shaped, like the Chiff-chaff's, and the materials used are similar. Up to eight eggs, carrying markings of a light red on a white ground, are laid. The parent birds are bold defenders of their nest, often disregarding their own safety.

Countless flies are devoured by the Willow Warbler, who also eats large numbers of other harmful insects. He is a good friend to man.

The bird is to be seen almost everywhere in these islands.

He leaves us during September.

THE WOOD WARBLER

THE NEAT and attractive Wood Warbler arrives in Britain a little later than his cousins, the Chiff-chaff and Willow Warbler. He leaves during September. Although the bird is fairly well spread throughout the British Isles, his fondness for trees keeps him to those districts in which woods and dense timbers abound.

The Wood Warbler, known also as the Wood Wren, is shy and reluctant to show himself, but a visit to an oak or beech wood – I would suggest the beech – may reward you with a sight of him high among the leaves. It is there that he hunts for his food, flitting from one tree to another in search of the insects which form his chief diet. Sometimes he pauses to pour out his song which, in the stillness of a beech wood, has a charm all its own.

He is a larger bird than the other two wrens – the Chiff-chaff and Willow Warbler – and he is more richly plumaged. Above he is coloured an attractive yellow-green; below, from throat to breast, a warmer yellow. Caught in a shaft of the sun the full beauty of the bird is brought out. He has a length of nearly 15 cm.

The nest of the Wood Warbler follows the pattern of the Chiff-chaff, being domed, and is placed in coarse grass on the ground, sometimes in a bank-side. The materials used are similar, except that feathers are not used as a lining. This is a point of identification worth remembering should you stumble on his nest. It receives, instead, a lining of fine grass and hair. Up to seven white eggs, splashed with markings of a purple-red, are laid in May.

THE REED WARBLER

A
S HIS name suggests, the Reed Warbler is a bird who spends much of his time among reeds. I have seen him along the upper reaches of the Thames, where the river is flanked by tall-growing reeds and sedges, and he is fairly common in most similar localities. The bird is a summer visitor and is generally with us by May, leaving in the autumn.

The general tone of the upper plumage is a warm chestnut-tinged brown; below he is buffish. The bird has a length of 14 cm.

The nest of the Reed Warbler, which diligent searching and the risk of wet feet, may reveal to you, has an interest particularly its own. As a rule it is situated in the depths of the reeds, where it is secured to three or four individual stems. By tying it in this way, the eggs in their deep, well-made nest, have a good chance of surviving severe disturbances among the reeds. In the building of the shell such materials as leaves and moss are used; the lining is usually of hair. Four, sometimes more, green-white eggs, mottled in a darker tone of the same colour, are laid early in June. Foster parentage is often forced on the parent birds by the Cuckoo. Water insects and worms picked up on the banks comprise the chief diet.

Although widely distributed throughout the British Isles, the Reed Warbler naturally keeps to those areas of marsh and riverside where reeds abound.

The Reed Warbler has many local names, but that of Marsh Reedling describes well the nature and habitat of this shy little waterside songster.

THE MARSH WARBLER

ALTHOUGH the Marsh and Reed Warblers so closely resemble each other as sometimes to baffle experienced naturalists, their habits differ quite widely. The Marsh Warbler has little use for reeds, preferring sedgy, swampy ground, or any stretch of dank water in which osiers grow. Nor is he so shy as his cousin. Once you have discovered his haunt it is not usually difficult to study his movements, though it probably will not be for intervals. Occasionally, during his stay with us, he leaves his osier bed on a brief foray to a field or coppice at hand. His song is superior to the Reed Warbler's, being clearer and sweeter. Customarily the bird makes his appearance here during May, sometimes later, and is off again in the early autumn.

Except that the legs of the Marsh Warbler are of a fleshy tint and are lighter in tone, and that his topcoat has less of the brown warmth of the Reed Warbler's, their colouring and general appearance are puzzlingly alike. The bird has a length of 14 cm.

The nest, which is made from grasses and moss, and a lining of hair, is generally constructed in a patch of dry ground, with a stream or stretch of water not too far off. Sometimes a low bush is used, but this, too, must be near water. Up to seven pale green-white eggs, marked in olive-brown, and mauve-grey, are laid in June.

The Marsh Warblers are few in number and breed mainly in the South of England. They come as spring visitors to this country.

THE SEDGE WARBLER

THE SEDGE WARBLER is another of the large family of warblers who come to spend the summer here. Sometime towards the end of April he crosses our shores and makes for some waterside splash of sedge or osier. Once settled in his haunt he shows himself as little as possible, though he makes known by his chattering song that he is not far off. At intervals he will forsake the cover of his osiers to search the surrounding terrain for food. It is at such moments that he presents the best view of himself, although, at the least disturbance he will quickly vanish.

The most noticeable feature of the Sedge Warbler is the yellow-white strip over the eye. Otherwise his upper plumage has a tawny tinge. A white chin and throat, and buff breast, complete the tones of his undercoat. The female's mantle is a duller edition of the male's. The bird has a length of 12 cm.

The fringe of the waterside or even a ditch is the site usually chosen for a nest, especially where the herbage is coarse and concealing. Bents, moss and grass form the walls of the nest, which is lined with hair and finer grasses, sometimes with an odd feather or two. Up to six pale brown eggs, carrying markings of a darker tone, are laid in May.

The bird lives chiefly on water insects and worms and, later in the year, berries are taken.

The Sedge Warbler is well spread about these islands, though it is less seen in the north.

His powers of mimicking the notes of other birds has earned him the local name of Mock Bird. He leaves us during the autumn.

THE GRASSHOPPER WARBLER

IT QUITE often happens that we know of the presence of certain birds only by hearing their call-note or song, for they rarely show themselves. This may be said of the Grasshopper Warbler, who is the shyest and most retiring of our warbler visitors. The singing notes of this bird bear some resemblance to the milling chirp of the grasshopper, and this, unless we exercise great caution and patience, may be the only indication we have that he is in the vicinity. Any area, especially if of a marshy nature, which offers plenty of dense cover, is acceptable to the Grasshopper Warbler, be it heath-land, plantation or even among the stems of ripening wheat. The bird arrives from his winter haunts abroad towards the end of April. He leaves again during September.

It is no easy task to find the nest of the Grasshopper Warbler as the sitting bird never flies off direct from her home. It is her practice to slip quietly off her eggs and make her way for some distance through the tangle of undergrowth before flying away to safety. The deep, well-like frame of the nest is fashioned from withered grasses. It has a lining of similar material, but of a finer texture. Up to six white, pink-tinged eggs, with markings of red-brown, are laid during May.

The plumage of the Grasshopper Warbler blends well with his green-tangled haunt. It is a brown-green above, and a light fawn below, the throat and breast being lightly marked with spots. The hen is very similar. The bird has a length of 14 cm.

The Grasshopper Warbler is an insect eater, and is fairly widely distributed throughout the British Isles.

THE HEDGE ACCENTOR

THIS QUIET little bird of the hedgerows is more commonly known as the Hedge Sparrow, a name which links him to the scallywag of the bird-world – the House Sparrow. Yet another name for him is the Hedge Warbler, and the pity is that it is not more widely used, for it is a happier choice and more in keeping with the bird's character. He has nothing in common with the Sparrow of our towns, except perhaps his general appearance.

Although he comes to our gardens and may be watched without much difficulty, he is really quite shy, giving the impression that he asks no more than to be left to live in his own way. In the early part of the year he is often to be seen about the leafless hedges, and his full liquid notes, which are then at their best quality, are very pleasant. His shuffling gait as he searches about the ground for food is a marked trait of this bird.

The Accentor's plumage is a homely brown tinged with red, with blue-grey throat and breast. The female's plumage is more faded. The bird has a length of 14 cm.

He conceals his nest with great care in some dense hedge or matted bush, but this provides no guarantee that it will escape the sharp eyes of the hen Cuckoo. For the Hedge Sparrow is the foster-parent most favoured by the Cuckoo and, more than any other bird, has to submit to the Cuckoo's unwanted attentions. As a nest-builder the Hedge Accentor is something of an artist. The nest is neatly woven of moss and twigs, lined with hair or wool. Up to six green-blue eggs, of a pastel richness, are laid in March.

Insects of many kinds are eaten by the Accentor, who is well dispersed about these islands.

THE GREAT TITMOUSE

SUCH SONG as the Great Titmouse emits during the early part of the year has the rasping quality of a file on rough metal, but as the season advances the notes become tuneful and cheery.

Although the natural haunt of this bird is the woodland and coppice, he may regularly be seen in orchards and gardens searching for insects and grubs. His quick, nimble ways are never without interest. Although he often damages the buds of fruit trees in his efforts to ferret out the destructive pests inside them, he is a good friend of the gardener and should be encouraged as a visitor.

His mantle is an attractive one and is not difficult to recognize, even though it bears some resemblance to the Blue Tit's. The crown of his head is blue-black. A small patch of white on the back of it abuts on to a topcoat of bright olive-green. The cheeks are white, the throat black. A further splash of black in the form of a band runs down the centre of the yellow breast. The female is not quite as colourful. The bird has a length of just under 15 cm.

The Great Titmouse can be readily tempted to set up his home in a nesting-box; indeed anything from a flower-pot to an old tin can will suit him, although a more natural site is a hole in a tree or wall. The nest is a cosy structure of mosses and grass warmly lined with hair, wool and feathers. Up to ten white eggs, marked in a light red, are laid in April.

Ox-eye is a well-known local name for this bird who, except for the North, is familiar to most parts of the British Isles.

THE BLUE TITMOUSE

THE BLUE TITMOUSE is one of the most colourful and certainly among the most popular of British birds. His pert and impish movements and comical acrobatics make him a welcome sight during the dour winter months when all our summer visitors have flown to warmer climes.

The Blue Tit is a busy little fellow, never still for a moment although he usually stays long enough in one place to enable you to take a good look at him. And it is worth while if only to see something of his colourful coat at short range. The rich blue crown is like an island in a channel of white. The white cheeks have a boundary of dark blue which cut into an eye-band of the same colour higher up. The throat is blue-black and the upper plumage a yellow-green. A blue-black line divides the yellow breast and belly. The hen bird is duller. The male bird's length is a little more than 10 cm.

The Blue Tit shares with his larger cousin, the Great Tit, the habit of making use of any suitable receptacle about the garden or elsewhere in which to make his nest. In woodlands he will usually choose a hole in a tree. The deserted home of a pair of Woodpeckers will suit him admirably. A lining of hair, wool and feathers goes into a moss-made shell. The Tom Tit, as he is also widely known, believes in large families. From seven to twelve eggs, sometimes more, are laid during April. They are white with faint red markings.

The Blue Tit is quite ready to pilfer a little fresh fruit, but his real food is the destructive insect.

There are few places in these islands where this sprightly fellow isn't known.

THE LONG-TAILED TITMOUSE

MANY Long-tailed Titmice are to be seen in woods on the outskirts of large towns, and a visit to almost any wooded glade during winter, when the birds are flitting about the trees in search of the insects, will be well repaid. But bird of the woodlands though he is, in the spring he makes for the hedges and bushes, there to begin the rearing of a family.

The Long-tailed Tit is a bird you cannot fail to recognize, since his tiny bill and very long black tail, edged with white, are two quite distinctive features. The white crown, throat and breast of his plumage, the black strip over the eye and rose-blurred belly are other points of identification. His length is about 14.5 cm.

The nest is a miracle of artistry. It is oval in shape and domed; it is built from lichens, wool and moss, with a lining of hair and massed feathers. The whole is woven together with gossamer spider's webs. A hole near the top is left for entering and leaving. How the bird disposes of his long tail in so small an area is explained by his habit of tucking it backwards over his body. In respect of the great number of feathers usually seen in these nests John Kearton, who examined a deserted one, writes: "I took it home and counted the feathers. There were 1,543."

Up to ten white eggs, more at times, slightly speckled in a brown-red, are laid during April.

The bird is found almost everywhere in these islands.

A familiar local name – one of many possessed by this bird – is Bottle Tit.

THE COAL TITMOUSE

THE COAL TITMOUSE keeps largely to the woodlands, a haunt suiting his quiet nature, for he is not nearly so bold and venturesome as the Blue Tit and Great Tit. Nevertheless, as autumn draws near, he sometimes shows up in gardens in the hope of finding some extra titbits of food. Insects which abound in trees are his usual fare but when, later in the year, seeds and nuts are to be had, he readily takes his fill of them.

A white patch on the back of the head of the Coal Tit is a feature to look for when identifying this bird: it is that part of his plumage which marks him out from the rest of the Titmice, especially from the Marsh Tit. The top part of his head and neck is black; the cheeks and neck-sides white. The breast is a blurred white, the belly buff-toned. He is 11 cm long.

During the first half of April the Coal Tit begins the task of nest-making. The site chosen is usually a hole in a tree; occasionally a crevice in a wall or bankside is preferred. Even the burrow of a mouse, as Howard Saunders tells us, is used. The main materials employed are dry grasses and moss and a lining of hair and wool. Up to ten white eggs, carrying markings of a pale red, are laid in April.

An apt local name for the bird is Coalhead.

The Coal Titmouse, while less common than the Blue Tit and Great Tit, is well dispersed about these islands.

THE MARSH TITMOUSE

I N AN earlier day the Marsh Titmouse spent much if not all of his time about fens and marshes. But many of these boggy wastes have now been drained, which may perhaps account for the fact that although he is still a frequenter of low-lying lands bounded by river or stream, he may also be seen in the fringes of woodlands, even in hedgerows, orchards and gardens.

It is easy, when looking for him, to confuse him with the Coal Tit, as in size and appearance the two birds are much alike, but he sports no white patch on the back of his head as does the Coal Tit. The upper parts of the head and neck are black; the plumage above is olive-brown, cheeks, throat and breast are a blurred white. The hen bird is similarly coloured. The male bird's length is about 11 cm.

The Marsh Tit is much attracted to the alder and willow, and he often sets up his nest in a hole in one of these trees. Sometimes the cavity chosen is not large enough for the birds' purpose, and on such occasions they do not hesitate to enlarge it themselves. John Kearton tells us : "The hole which these two particular birds (Marsh Tits) were working on was several inches in depth but after enlarging it for two or three days they abandoned their task and I saw them no more."

The materials used are moss and wool with a lining of down. Up to eight white eggs, with red-brown markings, are laid during April.

The bird confines himself to England and is very local in character. He and the Crested Tit are the least common of the Large Titmouse family. Insects form his main diet.

CRESTED TITMOUSE

THIS HANDSOME little member of the Titmouse family, who shares with the rest of his cousins their nimble ways and habits, is in other respects quite distinctive. He is much rarer than any other of the tits. He has little or no interest in man, and seldom leaves his timbered stronghold. He lives his life removed from the more common challenges to his safety and is able to breed without too much interference from enemies. England hardly knows him, and it is to the pine forests of Scotland that we must travel if we wish to get a glimpse of him in his natural haunts. Here, among the tall pines, the Crested Tit may be seen foraging about the branches in search of insects. Later in the year seeds and berries are included in his diet.

Only a little more than 10 cm in length, the Crested Tit is plumaged in olive-brown, with a whitish face and black patch below the chin. The throat and higher breast are black, the belly is grey-tinged white. The crest, which names the bird, and which adds a touch of novelty to his appearance, is black with grey-white fringes.

Howard Saunders says that the nest is: "generally placed in the rotten stump of a fir broken off by the wind; a hole being bored in the tree, from 60-240 cm from the ground; or in old stumps of very large trees within 14 cm of the soil. . . The usual materials are moss, wool and fur felted together. The eggs, from five to eight in number, are white, boldly spotted and zoned with light red."

When family cares are over and the winter draws in, a few Crested Tits are sometimes seen in company of more familiar birds.

THE GOLDEN-CRESTED WREN

THE GOLDEN-CRESTED WREN is a midget of the bird-world, being the smallest of British birds – a mere 9 cm in length. But though he is small he is hardier than many much larger in size. Nor does he lack colour in appearance. His crest is of rich lemon yellow deepening to a warm orange, and his topcoat of olive-green heightened by yellow, is plumage one might expect to see in a bird from the tropics. The dress of the hen bird is less colourful.

The Golden-crested Wren is an artist in nest-making. The deep and roomy cup which forms the shell is made from fine moss and lichens, which are skilfully interwoven in a smooth, felt-like mass. A warm, downy lining of feathers completes the work. A clutch of eggs, laid during April and May, may number up to ten. They are yellow-white in tone and carry red-brown markings at the wider end.

The haunt of the Golden-crested Wren is the fir forest, and it is here, beneath the branch of some favourite spruce fir, that the nest is usually situated.

Except when on the move in flock-flight, the bird is not often seen away from his woodland haunt, although he may make an occasional visit to some garden in the neighbourhood. He sings as he works – a quiet, pleasing little song.

Insects form the main food of this bird, who is well spread throughout the British Isles.

A local name which suits him is that of Wood Titmouse, but he is most commonly known as the Gold Crest.

THE WREN

PERHAPS because of his diminutive size or because of his jaunty carriage the Wren has a secure place in the affection of all bird-lovers. He is not so small as the Gold-crest, nor so fearless as the Robin, yet there is that about him which assures him a welcome wherever he goes. He is no stranger to gardens although he does not regularly advertise his presence by exposing himself to full view. Most of his time he spends in the lower branches of bushes and shrubs, attracting himself to the eye only by his quick, staccato movements as he hops from branch to branch. A much surer indication of his presence is his habit of breaking into song at almost any season of the year. At such times his song is a strong, pleasing trill, hardly believable from so small a frame. It is at its best about the middle of March.

There is nothing exotic about the colouring of the Wren. Its warmest note is rufous brown; a buff-white chin and throat merge into a breast and belly of a darker shade. The plumage of the female closely resembles the male's. The cock Wren measures a little more than 9 cm.

Nesting starts early – sometimes in March – and the site chosen may be a hedge, shrub, hay-stack or similar place. The nest is dome-shaped and is usually built from the materials he finds in the vicinity. Up to eight white eggs, sometimes more, carrying markings of red, are laid. The bird has the habit of constructing more nests than he needs.

There are few places in these islands where the popular little Wren is not known. He feeds almost exclusively on the insects and grubs he finds on the under-branches of hedgerows and shrubs.

THE KINGFISHER

ABOUT the waterways of the countryside there are no birds more beautiful than the Kingfisher. Certainly, none can surpass the colours of his coat. Wherever there's a river, stream or pool – or even a wayside ditch – you may hope to see him. Sometimes he will sit motionless on a stream-side perch for a minute or two before diving; an instant later he will disappear below the surface of the water in a flash of brilliant turquoise.

The Kingfisher is an expert fisherman, rarely returning from a dive without a struggling fish in his long bill. Then he will fly back to his perch and go through the surprising performance of tossing his prize into the air several times before gulping it down head first. Sometimes he varies his diet with beetles and other water creatures, but it is on small fish that he principally lives, a fact that has caused him to be persecuted on some rivers.

His plumage is vividly colourful – he is a veritable feathered jewel. Any attempt to do justice in words to his colouring would be wasted effort; suffice it to say that the general tones are blue-green, azure and orange. He has a length of 19 cm.

The Kingfisher is not at all nest-proud. A hole in a bank is the usual site. There is a lining, if such it can be called, of fish bones regurgitated by the birds. In this unattractive nursery are laid, during March, about seven, sometimes more, round, glossy-white eggs.

The Kingfisher is no songster, but his trilling whistle strikes a pleasing note in the hush of a rural backwater.

THE DIPPER

A FOAM-FLECKED, boulder-strewn mountain stream is the natural haunt of the Dipper. Now and again you may come across a pair of these attractive birds in the vicinity of a river or stream of a more placid character, but generally the Dipper revels in eddying, fast-moving water.

It is chiefly about the rivers of the North, standing on a rounded boulder in mid-stream, that the Dipper is most likely to offer a view of himself. There, if he is not disturbed, you will see him suddenly cut beneath the water in search of the river creatures on which he lives.

Naturalists have always been interested in this bird which, while having the form of a land-bird, wrests his living from under the water. I have watched him carefully on many occasions, and have never ceased to marvel at the remarkable way in which he propelled himself about the bed of the river, using his wings in the manner of fins.

The up-turned tail, brown-black topcoat, white chin, throat and breast, will leave no doubts in your mind as to the identity of the Dipper. His length is about 16.5 cm.

The nest of the Dipper, or Water Ousel as he is also known, may be concealed in a fissure between two boulders; or in a bank or beneath a bridge. It is dome-shaped and neatly made from moss, with a lining of leaves and grass. Up to six white eggs are laid during April. At least two broods are reared.

His food is the various insect and soft-shelled life to be found in water. He sings a quiet, tuneful melody, at its best in the early spring.

THE PIED FLYCATCHER

A BIRD of interest and appeal is the beautiful Pied Flycatcher, who makes the long journey each year from his African winter home to spend the summer with us. He is seldom here before the end of April, and usually leaves during September. Although scarcer than his cousin, the Spotted Flycatcher, the black and white bird is fairly often encountered because of his visits to orchards and gardens. Other areas he haunts are woodlands, especially those which flank a stretch of water.

Most of his food he takes in mid-air, swooping upon his prey like a small hawk. Even so there are those who say that he is less active as a hunter than the Spotted Flycatcher. The few notes he utters have little to commend them in the way of song but are not unpleasing.

His sharply-divided coat of blacks and whites is not easy to overlook, being black above and white below. The female is more quietly clothed in browns and duller whites. The bird is 13 cm in length.

The Pied Flycatcher's usual nesting-site is a tree-hole ; but he has a fondness for old stonework and masonry, in a crevice of which he will build his nest. The bird often returns to the nesting place of a year before. The materials used vary. Sometimes it will be of roots and grass, at others bents and moss or leaves and hair. Usually there is a lining of hair or hair and feathers. The eggs of this attractive bird are a delicate blue, of which up to eight are laid between May and June. At least one family is reared.

The bird is thinly distributed about these islands, favouring the North and West in which to breed.

THE BEARDED TITMOUSE

TIME WAS when great areas of fenland, rich in bird life, extended into several counties. As the marshes were drained and the land changed its character, the birds had to seek refuge elsewhere. In this manner the fenlands of Norfolk have become one of the few sanctuaries now remaining to certain breeds of birds.

Among these is the Bearded Titmouse, once a fairly common bird but now comparatively rare. It is found only in the neighbourhood of the Broads. The Bearded Titmouse, known also as the Bearded Reedling, is a difficult bird to locate and watch, for, apart from the fewness of his numbers, he is extremely shy and reveals himself for only the briefest moments as he moves about the dense reeds.

Writing of this bird, E. W. Hendy says: "Your first acquaintance with it is likely to be a glimpse of a small bird with a long, chestnut tail, flitting over the tops of the withered reeds and disappearing suddenly into them."

The two wispy feathers which hang below the eye of this bird and form his "beard" are his chief point of interest, but his rich tawny-orange coat and long, fan-shaped tail are very pleasing to the eye. He has a length of 16.5 cm.

Nest-making is begun during the first half of April. The cup-shaped shell is formed from withered reeds and sedges, which receive a lining of feathery reed-tops. Up to six white eggs, sometimes more, lightly marked in black, are laid. The bird is fond of watersnails, and insects of all kinds. His call-note is a clear, oft-repeated *Ping*.

THE SPOTTED FLYCATCHER

THE SPOTTED FLYCATCHER has a fondness for gates and posts on which to perch, and it is from these that often he hawks food, making sudden flashes into the air the moment he spots his quarry. It is difficult to discover whether he ever misses his prey, but so sure are his judgment and speed, it cannot be often that he does. Having caught his prize, he flies back to his perch, and takes up his position for the next pounce.

As well as making gardens his headquarters, he spends much of his time in woodlands. Some Spotted Flycatchers often reach the United Kingdom before April is out, but most of them defer their visit until the early part of May, leaving again during September. This quiet little brown bird is silent and songless as he waits to dart from his perch. The few notes that he utters from time to time are quite unremarkable.

Nature has mantled him in a sober brown coat above and a near-white one below. The throat and breast carry the brown markings which give him the "Spotted" part of his name. He has a length of 14 cm.

The bird varies his choice of nesting-site. Sometimes it is a hole in a tree, sometimes against the trunk, sometimes a well-screened leafy wall will be chosen, and occasionally he will pick on a barn or shed. The nest is usually cup-shaped and is made from moss, lichens and webs, with a lining of hair and feathers. The four to five eggs laid in May have a bluish tinge with speckles of rust-red.

The Spotted Flycatcher is widely distributed about the wooded areas of the British Isles.

THE PIED WAGTAIL

BIRD GRACE at its best may be seen in the wagtail family; and the Pied Wagtail, although lacking the richer colour of his cousins, is a handsome and striking member of it. It is a remarkable experience to watch these birds snatch up insects and grubs from behind a moving plough: it is interesting, too, to see them running in the light-stepping manner characteristic of their kind through the grasses by the water's edge, every now and then making little leaps into the air to catch flies and small moths. The Pied Wagtail trills a few pleasing notes during the spring.

My garden is regularly visited by Pied Wagtails. They are less confiding than the Starlings, Blackbirds, thrushes and others who come there, but if you don't disturb them they will stay and feed from the lawn quite happily. Strangely the male and female rarely appear together. One day the cock bird will show up; the next day comes the hen.

The Pied Wagtail wears a spick and span uniform of blacks and whites, his long, ever-flicking tail edged with white. The hen bird is less sharply coloured. The male has a length of about 19 cm.

Like the Robin and some of the Tits, the Pied Wagtail will sometimes set up his nest in unusual places, but generally he chooses a site among the lush grasses of a wayside stream. Roots, moss and grasses form the shell ; the lining is of hair and feathers or wool. Up to six grey-white, ash-brown speckled eggs are laid during April. The nest is much favoured by the Cuckoo.

The Pied Wagtail is to be met with throughout these islands.

THE GREY WAGTAIL

ALL THE wagtails have long, streamlined tails, but the Grey Wagtail has the longest of them all. He is a most beautiful bird who, seen by some tumbling mountain stream, presents a picture not soon forgotten. In common with the other wagtails, the "Grey" has but little song.

The Grey Wagtail, like the Dipper, earns his living from the running waters of unfrequented streams, taking from them insects, beetles and small snails. In quick staccato movements he darts from boulder to boulder, leaving them for short periods to paddle in the shallows and pick up morsels of food.

The plumage of this bird is comprised of blue-greys and yellows, attractively offset by a rich black throat. He is about 19 cm in length.

During nesting-time frequent journeys to and from the nest by the parent birds may betray its position to the observer, but otherwise the nest is exceedingly difficult to find. Usually it is placed where it blends into the surroundings, sometimes under, the leaves of an overhanging bank, sometimes on a concealed rocky ledge. The nest is seldom far from water. Moss, bents and roots and a hair lining go into the making of the cup-shaped nest. Up to five grey-white eggs, with light-brown mottlings, are laid during April.

The Grey Wagtail is well dispersed about the British Isles.

The bird's tail-flicking trait gives rise to one of several local names – Grey Wagster.

THE YELLOW WAGTAIL

I T IS the habit of this very colourful bird to follow closely on behind cattle and snap up the insects disturbed by the hooves. At such times, he is so nimble and venturesome that he darts almost under the descending hoofs of the moving herd. But although the Yellow Wagtail goes to the fields for much of his food, his real haunt is in the vicinity of marsh and water; and it is from the water-mead that he claims a large part of his diet. He is a welcome summer visitor, although he is less known in the North, settling himself mostly in the Midlands and Southern Counties. He is usually here during the first half of April and leaves in September.

The coat of this bird is a very smart one of yellow-tinged olive above, and rich yellow below, but he is a smaller bird than the others of his family, his length being a little more than 15 cm.

The nest is generally built on the ground, usually very cleverly concealed among the lush grasses of a water-meadow. Occasionally, however, the sprouting stems of growing corn or beneath the leaves of turnips will be accepted as a suitable nesting-site. The materials employed are grasses and moss for the frame, wool and feathers or down for the lining. Up to six grey-white, clay-brown mottled eggs are laid sometime between May and July.

The local name of Cow Bird expresses the habit of this Wagtail to follow cattle in pursuit of insects.

THE BLUE-HEADED WAGTAIL

ANOTHER handsome member of the wagtail family is the Blue-headed Wagtail; but although he comes here regularly each spring, he does so in meagre numbers. He usually heads for the Eastern parts of England. On account of the scarcity of this bird the chances of seeing him in his haunt are slender. Often his visits are only transitory, but if he does stay to breed here, he chooses a site similar to that favoured by the other members of the wagtail clan.

Like the Yellow Wagtail, whom he closely resembles, he is a great hunter of the insects which hover about cattle and horses, and is no less venturesome in his efforts to swoop them up. Howard Saunders remarks on this: "The food consists of insects and their larvae; and the bird is very partial to small flies, in pursuit of which it may be seen fluttering within a few inches of the muzzles of grazing cattle and horses."

The mantle of the Blue-headed Wagtail is a richly-painted one. His blue-grey head flanks a topcoat of yellow-tinged olive; below, the white note of the chin is caught up in the throat and breast of bright yellow. The strip running over the eye is white, a point to bear in mind should you by some lucky accident stumble on him. Otherwise he and the Yellow Wagtail are confusingly alike.

The Blue-headed Wagtail lays up to six eggs – the materials for the nest being similar to the Yellow Wagtail's.

THE TREE PIPIT

SOME BIRDS, although of the same family and alike in appearance and general ways, sometimes differ from each other by some oddity of habit. This can be said of the Tree Pipit who, while living in many respects the life of the Meadow Pipit, prefers to perch in trees rather than settle on the ground.

The haunt of the Tree Pipit is the woodland, and it is from the topmost branches of a tree that he soars aloft and, having reached the limit of his upward flight, drops with upturned tail spiralling back to his perch. During this performance he sometimes trills a short song and he will often continue to sing his notes after he has returned to his perch. He is not, like the Meadow Pipit, a resident bird, but comes as a visitor each year, usually arriving by the second week of April. He prefers the Southern areas of these islands, over which he is widely distributed. He lives on insects and seeds.

The Tree Pipit is coloured in warm browns above; below, the chin is a blurred white, the throat, neck and breast buff. He is 15 cm long.

The nest is usually placed on the ground. Grass, moss, and a lining of finer grasses are the materials used. The eggs vary both in their base colour and in their markings. Some have a warm red-brown, others a ground tone of clay-white with a clouded surface of grey-browns. The task of deciding the owner of such variously-coloured eggs is no easy one! Up to six are laid between April and May.

THE MEADOW PIPIT

TITLARK is the name by which this bird is more widely known, especially in those parts of the country where he is most in evidence. The Meadow Pipit is at home in most open country, being equally as content in lush meadows, where he may be seen tripping along in the dainty manner of the wagtails, as in the bleaker territory of the moors.

The song of the Meadow Pipit lacks the sweetness of the Tree Pipit's but he has the same habit of uttering his notes when it flight, usually as he descends. In the winter the Meadow Pipits join together in flocks. There are few places in the British Isles where he is not to be seen. Insects, worms and seeds are eaten in large quantities. He is certainly a good friend to man.

The topcoat worn by this bird is brown, with an olive tinge ; below he is coloured dull buff-white spotted with dark brown from the throat to the lower breast. His length is 14.5 cm.

The nest, hidden by scrub or tall grasses, is constructed on the ground ; on moors heather is used for protective cover. Every effort is made to conceal the nest, but the Cuckoo will not overlook it, the homes of Meadow Pipits being often visited. The shell of the nest is usually put together with coarse grasses, fine ones being used for the lining, sometimes hair. Up to six eggs are laid between April and May, the more general tones of which are red-brown. Two families are reared.

THE RED-BACKED SHRIKE

SMALL birds and nestlings of the woodlands have good cause to fear the predatory Red-backed Shrike. His habit of impaling his victims on thorns has earned him the ugly name of Butcher Bird. But he does not confine himself to birds with which to stock his larder; mice, shrews, voles, large insects, beetles and wasps – all are taken to satisfy his hunger.

You may see him perched on a wayside telegraph wire as though quietly taking his rest. Then quite suddenly he will swoop down on his unsuspecting prey. A deadly blow from behind with his powerful beak and one more victim is whisked off and skewered on a thorn near his nest.

The Red-backed Shrike is a summer visitor who arrives here towards the end of April or beginning of May and leaves before August is out. He keeps himself to the wooded areas of the Midland and Southern Counties.

The plumage of this hawk-like little bird – he is no longer than 18 cm – is a colourful one. The grey crown and neck run into a warm, brown-red back. Except for the white chin the lower mantle is a rose-buff.

The centre of a thick and thorny hedge is his choice for a nest, which is made from twigs, dry grass, moss and wool, and receives a lining of fine roots. In form it is cup-shaped. The eggs, of which up to six are laid during May, vary in colour, but the commonest are splashed with grey about the larger end, the ground colour varying between a green-white and grey-white. One family is reared.

THE SKYLARK

MY GARDEN abuts on to a farm, from the fields of which I have seen many Skylarks soar upwards into the clear blue of a summer sky. Many times, too, have I listened to the delightful music which he makes as he flies higher and higher until he is no longer visible. To enable him to achieve such lofty ascents Nature has given to the Skylark great length of wing and, for the ground, where he spends much of his time, great length of claw. The haunts of this bird, who is a familiar figure throughout these islands, are mainly open pasture, from which he gets his living in the form of insects of all kinds and, later in the year, seeds.

A songster of such quality deserves perhaps a more colourful coat, but the warmest tints the Skylark can muster are a tinge of golden-brown above and fawny-white below. He wears a light strip over the eye. He is 18 cm in length.

Many eggs must be lost to Skylarks every year on account of their habit of placing their nests in open fields. Even though the nests are cunningly concealed and the parent birds resort to all kinds of deceptive tactics to lead the intruder from the vicinity of the nest, winged and four-footed robbers reap a rich harvest in eggs and fledglings. Any patch in a field offering a screen of tangled grasses may be selected as a nest-site, and here in a shallow hollow in the ground a nest of coarse grass with a lining of softer material will be built. Up to five grey-white eggs, thickly marked in a deeper grey or olive-brown, are laid early in May.

THE WOODLARK

THE WOODLARK is a smaller edition of the Skylark and, being much scarcer, is less often to be seen. He keeps to certain areas of the country, generally in the South, and for this reason he is unknown in some districts altogether. In Scotland he is seen only on rare occasions.

The song of the Woodlark lacks the range and variation of the Skylark's, but he makes up for that by the sweetness and liquid quality of his notes. He sings when on the wing as well as on the ground, and may frequently be heard as the day is ending, at times even at night. His haunts are mainly the fringes of woodlands, particularly those which flank wild, open land.

His manner of returning from a song-flight differs from the Skylark's in that the Woodlark's is spiral as opposed to the diagonal descent of the Skylark. He is an insect-eater but he will readily accept seeds.

Except that the light strip over the eye is broader and more pronounced in the Woodlark, and his tail shorter, the plumage of Woodlark and Skylark is confusingly alike. The main point of distinction between the two birds is one of size. The Woodlark is 15 cm in length.

A chance shallow in the ground, screened by herbage, or in a tussock of grass itself, is the usual nesting-site. It is a compact nest made chiefly from bents and grasses and lined with finer grasses. Towards the second half of March a first clutch of up to five off-white eggs with markings of red-brown, is laid. Two families are normal during the breeding season.

THE SWALLOW

O F OUR many bird visitors the handsome Swallow is probably more widely known than the others. He is the visitor we look forward to as the herald of summer. He is usually with us by the third week in April, and the sharply forked tail and drawn back wings as he skims gracefully over a placid pool or across a meadow are as familiar a sight about the outskirts of towns as in rural areas. Now and again the bird pauses in his labours to take up a perch on a handy bough or telegraph wire, there to render his few trilling notes. There must be few places in these islands where the Swallow may not be seen though he is less numerous in the North. The bird hawks the insects he eats on the wing.

The rich metal-blue of the Swallow's topcoat, which is broken here and there by greens, brings out the very pleasing tones of the under-mantle. The forehead patch and throat are of chestnut, the belly a warm buff. He has a length of 19 cm.

Country folk know the bird as the Chimney Swallow because of his use of the inside ledges of chimneys for nesting; but he is just as liable to set up home under a bridge, in a barn or in any other convenient spot. He often returns to the same nest each year. The nest, which is built from mud, hay and straw, is saucer-shaped and is lined with feathers. From four to six white, grey-brown speckled eggs are laid in May. At least two families are reared.

The Swallows leave during the first half of October when large numbers may be seen together about reed-beds, roofs, trees and other places.

THE SWIFT

SO FAST and powerful is the Swift in flight that at times it is difficult to follow his aerial movements. One moment you have him within the arc of your vision, in the next he has disappeared in the vastness of the skies. He will swoop from a great height with incredible speed in his search for winged insects and will continue to do so tirelessly throughout the day. A peculiarity of this bird is the construction of its claws, which will not permit it to perch in the manner of other birds. Rather does it have to cling to the branch or telephone wire on which it is resting. For the same reason the Swift is almost helpless when on the ground and can only move around in the most clumsy fashion.

The Swift is one of our later visitors, coming during the first week in May and generally leaving about the middle of August. A few pairs sometimes linger on till the first half of September. He is well distributed about these islands.

A small patch of near-white under the chin is the one contrasting colour-note; otherwise the plumage is a uniform brown-black. The bird has a length of 16.5 cm.

The Swift collects the materials for his nest as he flies around. Usually these are straws, hay and feathers which, when made into the shell, are held together with a tacky spittle. A favourite nesting-site is under the eaves of houses; but cliffs and similar places are used. Two, sometimes three, white eggs are laid towards the end of May or early in June.

The shrill scream of the Swift has earned him a local name of Screecher.

THE HOUSE MARTIN

SOON AFTER the Swallow has arrived we may expect another member of the same family – the House Martin. He is as familiar a sight as the larger bird and is often mistaken for him. But you will notice that his tail is shorter. During his stay he takes up his residence in almost every part of the British Isles. He leaves in October.

The House Martin will often hunt higher in the air for insects than the Swallow, or he may, low over the ground or the surface of a stretch of water, hunt on the same purpose. The Martin is able to cling to a sheer wall without difficulty, and will often do so for long periods of time, with nothing but his grappling claws and sturdy tail to support him. He has a low, pleasing twitter.

There is a rich sheen on the blue-black topcoat of the House Martin. His rump is splashed with a small area of white, which is absent in the Swallow – and his under-surface is an unbroken white where the Swallow's is definitely buff. He is about 14 cm in length.

The nest-building of the House Martin is quite distinctive. It is a shell of mud erected with patient labour chiefly beneath the eaves of a roof. Many journeys are made to collect the mud, which is built up very gradually until it joins the eave. A hole is left by which the birds enter and leave. There is a lining of hay and feathers. Up to five white eggs are laid during May. At least two families are reared.

A local name aptly describing the appearance of this bird is White-rumped Swallow.

THE SAND MARTIN

ALTHOUGH the Sand Martin, smallest of the Swallow family, is sometimes with us before the boisterous winds of March have blown themselves out, he usually arrives during the first week in April. By the end of September he is gone again.

Where there is sand that is not too near human dwellings the Sand Martin will readily settle and rear a family. He likes the company of his kind, and it is quite usual to see large colonies of these birds nesting together. Sand Martins are spread about these islands in those districts suited to their way of life. They live largely on insects. Their few singing notes are pleasing but not strong.

It should not be difficult to recognize this small bird – he is just under 13 cm in length – as his upper mantle lacks the colour depth of his two cousins, the Swallow and House Martin, being of a mouse-like tone of brown. His under plumage is mainly white.

The grapnel-like claws and short, sharp bill of the Sand Martin are well suited to the tunnelling of sand; and these enable him to dig down to a depth of two or more feet when burrowing out a nesting-site. He begins by scraping a small hole in the surface with his bill and this he enlarges until he is able to stand in it and use his claws. Male and female share the work. When the required depth has been mined, a larger space is cleared for the living chamber. This is lined with bents and feathers. Up to six white eggs are laid during April. Two families are reared. When nesting is over the birds often resort to stretches of water.

THE NIGHTJAR

THE GORSE common and moorland with their dense herbage are the haunts favoured by the Nightjar, whose ashy-grey plumage, barred and spotted in brown, is very difficult to pick out from his immediate surroundings. It is towards the evening, when he leaves his day-time shelter to hunt for food, that you can see this very interesting bird at work. He is a summer visitor who lands here about the second week in May and leaves before September is out. Nightjars are thinly dispersed about these islands.

The silent, bat-like flight of the Nightjar and his habit of hunting at dusk are two traits this bird has in common with the owl. But his method of feeding is more like that of the Swallow and Swift, swooping upon his prey in mid-flight. His diet is mainly moths and beetles. His flight is as restless and agile as the Swift's. One moment he will be wheeling, the next soaring, closely following every twist and turn of the prey he is pursuing. Occasionally he will bring his wings together in a clapping motion, emitting at the same time an air-suck type of whistle.

When at rest he sits in a lengthwise position, and it is at such times that he utters the curious churring note peculiar to his kind.

The Nightjar has no interest in nest-building: the two white, brown-mauve marked eggs are laid in the bare bracken during June.

Countrymen of an earlier day, ever fond of attributing to certain birds strange and unlikely habits, christened him Goatsucker. There is of course no evidence to support this curious belief.

His length is about 25 cm.

THE GREEN WOODPECKER

COMING from the woodlands at the back of my house I often hear a note unlike any other uttered by our wild birds. It is the clear, loud, laugh-like call of the Green Woodpecker, or Yaffle as he is also known.

The instinct for ferreting out decay in trees and the wood-boring insects it harbours is strong in the Woodpecker family, and the Green Woodpecker, largest of the three Woodpeckers which reside with us, is no exception. The powerful, hammering beak explores every crack and crevice in its search for food, digging deep into the rotting wood with relentless efficiency. The bird is also very fond of ants, feeding on vast quantities when he has the fortune to come across a colony.

Another purpose to which the Woodpecker's probing beak is put is the boring of a nesting-site. In this he cuts a beautifully symmetrical hole in a suitable tree trunk, lining it with no more than a few wood-chips. In these secure if austere surroundings, the five to seven glossy-white eggs are laid in April.

Plumage as colourfully attractive as the Green Woodpecker's adds greatly to the interest of this bird. The top mantle begins with a crimson crown and neck, running into a back of olive green and a rump of rich yellow. Below are black cheeks and a light grey-green breast and belly. This handsome bird has a length of 30 cm.

The Green Woodpecker, whose haunt is the woodland, is chiefly to be met with in the timbered areas of England and Wales.

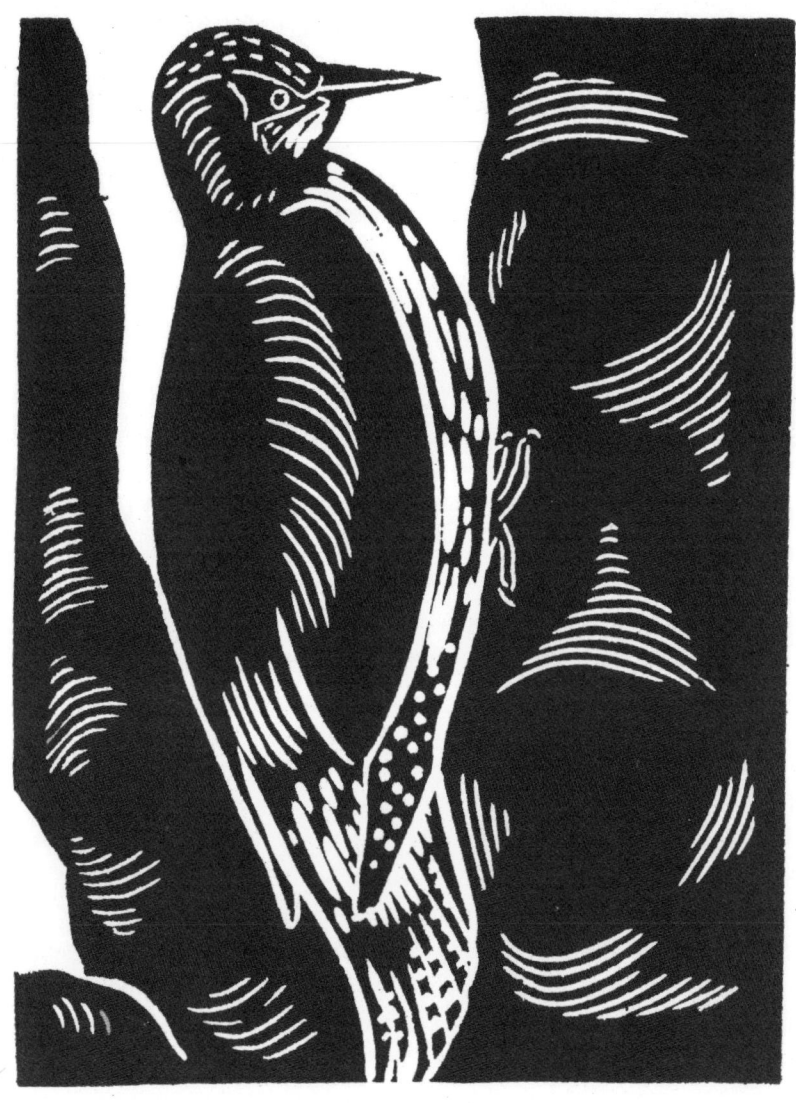

THE GREAT SPOTTED WOODPECKER

THIS VERY attractive member of the Woodpecker family does not announce his presence by shrill and echoing note in the manner of the Green Woodpecker. Indeed, except when he's at work drumming against a tree-trunk, he's almost silent. He is a shy creature, unwilling to expose himself to human gaze and quick to dodge round to the far side of a tree-trunk or shelter behind a screen of foliage at the approach of man. Only when he is quite certain that the intruder has gone, will he reappear and get back to the day's work. Of the three Woodpeckers inhabiting the British Isles, the Great Spotted Woodpecker is the rarest. This fact, allied to the natural shyness of the bird, and his habit of keeping well aloft in a tree, makes him a bird not often seen by the casual observer. But with care and patience it is possible to take him unawares and at such times he shows himself to be well worth watching. Wood-boring insects and, later in the year, berries and nuts are his main food.

The plumage of the Great Spotted Woodpecker is a bright and colourful one of barred blacks and whites and crimsons. On the back of the head, between the black crown and black body, is a band of crimson. The lower body has a splash of crimson, a strip of which runs beneath the tail. He has a length of 24 cm.

The nesting-hole bored by this Woodpecker is usually deeper and smaller than that of the Yaffle. Now and again a ready-made hole will be used. Up to seven glossy-white eggs are laid during May.

Scotland and Ireland see very little of the Great Spotted Woodpecker but many of England's quiet woodlands know this attractive and interesting bird. Pied Woodpecker is one of the many local names by which this bird is also known.

THE LESSER SPOTTED WOODPECKER

ONE OF the most interesting and remarkable features of all the Woodpeckers is the clever use they make of claws and tail as they hammer into the bark of a tree. The needle-like claws bite firmly into the trunk, and the stiff, sturdy tail-feathers are bent partially under the body and pressed against the tree-side to give extra support and stability. In this position the bird has full freedom of movement, and the stabbing bill can work at top pressure. The tongue of the Woodpecker, too, is of peculiar interest. A. R. Thompson, who has closely studied these birds, writes: "The tip of the tongue is provided with a few sharp barbs and the whole tongue is covered with a sticky secretion of which there is an abundant supply in the salivary glands. Large insects are impaled on the barbed tip; smaller fry is held by means of the gummy nature of the tongue. The Woodpecker is thus well able to extract wood-boring insects from their tunnels."

The Lesser Spotted Woodpecker is quite a little fellow compared to his larger cousins, the Green and Great Spotted Woodpeckers, but he is no less attractive or interesting. Like the Great Spotted Woodpecker he is of a very retiring nature and he has the same shy habit of remaining in the upper branches of the trees. Thus it is necessary to approach with great caution if one hopes to get a sight of him as he goes about his business of extracting insects from the boughs of his woodland home.

In a bare nesting-hole which he bores go the four to five white eggs. His plumage is a dapper one. Crimson crown, black neck, barred black and white wings are above; below it is a buff-white. He is 14 cm in length.

The bird lives chiefly in the wooded areas of England and Wales.

THE WRYNECK

THE COINCIDENT arrival of the Wryneck and Cuckoo has been responsible for dubbing the Wryneck "The Cuckoo's Mate." In spite of this, the Wryneck has nothing in common with the Cuckoo either in habit, plumage or appearance. In many ways he is closer akin to the woodpeckers and, like them, feeds largely on the various insects which infest trees. Ants, too, may form a major part of his diet. The Wryneck is a cautious bird which will flit off at the least disturbance, and because of his plumage, which blends so well into the surroundings, he is difficult to keep in sight.

By the second week in April he is usually with us, landing as a rule a day or two ahead of the Cuckoo. He leaves for his winter home overseas before September is out. While here he keeps mainly to the Southern and South-Eastern parts of England.

Compared to the colouring of our woodpeckers the plumage of the Wryneck is drab, but there is a certain richness about the markings and mottlings of brown, grey and black which is of a pleasing quality. The bird has a length of 18 cm.

The Wryneck usually nests in a tree-hole, though he does not bore it himself. He prefers to take possession of a natural cavity in which, about the second week of May, is laid a clutch of up to ten white eggs. Intruders to the nest, whether human, furred or feathered, are discouraged by snake-like hisses and no less serpentine writhings and twistings of the neck. This behaviour has earned him a local name of Snake-bird. The same hole is often returned to year after year.

The bird has a shrill call-note, but no song.

THE TREE CREEPER

WHEN WALKING through woodlands it is no uncommon thing to see a brown-backed creature running mouse-like about the trunk of a tree. Closer examination will betray the neat white front and curved bill of the Tree Creeper. This bird will move with astonishing speed in search of its food up the perpendicular face of a tree. Its diet consists of the insects it finds in the bark, and for this purpose it would be difficult to devise a more useful probe than the bill of this bird, which resembles a tiny pick-axe.

The Tree Creeper shows little fear of man. I have many times sat at the foot of a tree and watched a Creeper going about his work above my head just as though I wasn't there.

His manner of hunting is to spiral up from the bottom of the tree, running quickly upward, stopping for a moment to snap up some insects, and then continuing until he has reached the limit of his climb. Then he will fly off to the next tree. During the nesting season his shrill little trill is often uttered as he moves about the tree-trunk.

The plumage of this quiet, useful little bird is a sharply divided one of brown and white. His back is of a warm brown, his chin, throat, breast and belly a snowy white. He is of about 13 cm in length.

A favourite nesting-site is in a natural hollow or in the cavity left by bark which has broken from the trunk. Beneath this sheltering roof is placed a nest of twigs and grass with a lining of bark-strips, feathers and moss.

Up to nine white eggs, with markings of red-brown, are laid during May. The bird may be met with throughout the British Isles.

THE NUTHATCH

A WALK into any beech wood may well take you into the haunts of the Nuthatch, and the chances are that if you see him he will be hanging upside down from a small branch. The grapnel-like grip of his claws enables him to take up almost any position in which to ferret out the insects he eats. Sometimes he will take seeds from the ground. During the autumn of the year when the nuts ripen and are plentiful, the Nuthatch spends much of his time breaking open the shells and extracting the kernels. With quite remarkable resource he will wedge a nut into a crevice of bark and then proceed to crack it open by a series of pounding hammer blows from his powerful bill.

The spring song of the bird is a clear, metallic trill of a few notes uttered at brief intervals. He is chiefly known in the woodlands of the Southern and Midland Counties of England.

The Nuthatch has a coat of many colours – pleasing colours. From the crown to the rump there is a run of delicate slate-blue; across the eye is a black strip. The mantle below begins with chin and cheeks of white which pass to a throat and belly of warm buff. He has a length of 14 cm.

A usual nesting-site is a tree-hole which the Nuthatch, having in mind both safety and privacy, plasters in until there is only room enough left by which to enter or leave. The nest is bedded out with leaves and a few bark strips. Up to seven white eggs, with red-brown markings, are laid in April or May.

A quaint local name is Nutjobber.

THE CUCKOO

THE CALL of the Cuckoo is the most familiar and easily recognized of all bird-notes. It resembles that of no other bird, and because the Cuckoo is popularly regarded as a harbinger of spring the notes of the first arrivals each year are eagerly awaited.

In the bird-world, however, the Cuckoo is far from popular. His hawk-like appearance is often the cause of smaller birds mobbing him on sight, and his parasitic habits do nothing to endear him to many human observers. He is usually here by the second week in April and is gone again before August is out. The season's young birds follow somewhat later. During the Cuckoo's stay, there are few woodlands in these islands where his familiar two notes are not to be heard. He is mainly an insect-eater. His plumage is ash-blue above, a barred white below. He is rather more than 30 cm in length.

The habit of the female Cuckoo of laying her eggs in the nests of other birds has ever been the cause of controversy among naturalists. Whether she lays it directly in the nest, or lays it in advance and deposits it there with her beak has been widely discussed but never definitely proved. What is certain is that the hatching of the young Cuckoo ends the chances of survival of the other young birds in the nest. Being much larger and stronger than the other nestlings it quickly ejects them one by one until it alone remains. The curious thing is that in spite of this murderous behaviour the foster-parents continue devotedly to feed the monster in their nest until he is able to fend for himself.

Some of the Cuckoo's favourite nesting victims are the Hedge Sparrow, Pied Wagtail, Meadow Pipit, Redbreast, Reed Warbler and Yellow Bunting. The Cuckoo's eggs vary in tone between a grey-green with darker markings and a light blue.

THE CHAFFINCH

THE CHAFFINCH is among the most numerous of British birds. Although he is by nature a bird of the fields and woodlands, he may still be quite frequently encountered in town gardens and parks many miles from the open countryside.

The Chaffinch is a colourful little bird, rarely shy of human beings, and often remarkably bold. Apart from the familiar *pink-pink* which he utters incessantly, he has a most pleasing song with which he entertains his world during the early summer.

In the matter of food, all is grist that comes to the Chaffinch's mill. He has the most catholic ideas about diet and will readily stuff himself with seeds of all kinds, with caterpillars, flies and moths, and with berries and garden fruit.

His coat is an attractive and colourful one. A black forehead borders a blue-grey crown and neck ; a warm red-brown back runs into a yellow-green rump; below, the cheeks, throat and breast are a chestnut-red. The upper wings carry a noticeable splash of white. He is about 15 cm in length.

The Chaffinch builds a beautiful cup-shaped nest, choosing any well-screened bush or shrub that offers protection and inaccessibility from the ground. Sometimes he will build in the fork of a tree. The nest is made of moss, lichens and wool which are finely woven together and lined with hair and feathers.

Up to six eggs are laid between April and May. The eggs vary somewhat in colour but are usually a pale blue-green with purple-brown markings. Two families are reared.

THE GREENFINCH

A S HIS name implies, the Greenfinch is another member of the large finch family. Like the Chaffinch he may frequently be seen in gardens although his more natural haunts are the woodlands. Shyer and less inclined to show himself than the friendly Chaffinch he may often be heard uttering his long-drawn, croon-like note from a hedge-top or other green clump, but quickly retires from view on being disturbed.

The Greenfinch is a ready robber of orchards and gardens and for this reason is sometimes not welcomed by gardeners. On the other hand he eats large quantities of insects and pests which attack fruit and growing crops, and the balance may be said to be in his favour. England, Wales, Scotland and Ireland know him well.

The Greenfinch is a well-groomed little bird, his colouring being made up of a wide variety of shades of green and yellow. His back is mainly olive-green with a strong yellow note near the rump. A pleasing touch of colour is the yellow-gold strip over the eye. The throat, breast and belly are a yellow-green, and his heavy beak has a flesh tint. In a shaft of sunlight the plumage has a most striking appearance. The bird has a length of 15 cm.

Sometimes the nest is built fairly high up in a tree or in a patch of ivy; but the more usual site is a hedge or bush. It comprises a loose framework of twigs, moss and grass, and is lined with hair. Up to six green-white eggs, with markings of brown or purple at the lower end, are laid between April and May.

In winter large flocks of Greenfinches rove the fields feeding from the seeds of weeds. A local name is Green Linnet, but he has not the Linnet's sweet song.

THE HAWFINCH

I T WAS in Epping Forest, many years back, that I saw my first Hawfinch. He was high up in the branches of a hornbeam, and through my binoculars I could study the stocky body and marvel at the massive beak which seemed out of all proportion to his size. He must have known that he was being watched, for a moment later he was gone. The Hawfinch is easily the shyest of the finches, and his whistle-like note is often the only clue to his presence. But his visits to gardens for peas and fruit offer occasional opportunities of seeing him for brief intervals.

His normal food consist of insects, seeds, berries and the stones of plum and cherry, which the hard knobs inside his bill crush with ease. He has no song worthy of the name. A resident bird, he keeps chiefly to his chosen districts in England.

His orange-brown head, grey neck and brown back, white-patched wings and light wine-coloured under-mantle give the Hawfinch an attractive appearance. He has a length of 18 cm.

He usually chooses a position high up in a tree, tall hedge or bush in which to build his nest. Twigs and roots, with a lining of twigs and hair, are the materials used. The eggs, of which up to six are laid in April or May, have a pleasing blue-green tone, broken by blotches and streaks of olive-grey or black. Only one family is reared.

The fondness of the bird for stone fruits has earned him a local name of Cherry Finch.

BULLFINCH

THE BULLFINCH does not normally court the society of man, but when the chance of fresh fruit comes his way he often loses his caution and shyness. In an orchard in Hertfordshire, where soft fruits are grown under large wire cages, I have seen half a dozen Bullfinches wait patiently until the door was opened, and then shoot in to raid the bushes. In the early part of the year the Bullfinch has an unfortunate habit of pecking out fruit buds, which has given him a bad name in some quarters, but he is also a great destroyer of harmful insects which do quite as much damage in their own way. He also eats large quantities of seeds and berries. Woodlands are the natural haunt of the Bullfinch, and he is to be met with almost everywhere in these islands.

One of the charms of this bird is his colourful coat. A silky blue-black head joins a slate-grey back and white-patched rump. These sober colours are offset by the bright brick-red cheeks and breast. The female is a less colourful bird. The male is 15 cm in length.

A favourite nesting-site is a thorn hedge, along a short strip of which several nests may sometimes be found. The nest is little more than a staging of twigs and a cup-like lining of roots and a little hair. Up to six pale green-blue eggs, carrying markings of brown-red and purple, are laid between April and May. At least one family is raised.

Some authorities believe that Bullfinches pair for life.

THE GOLDFINCH

B IRDS of bright and colourful plumage are not uncommon in the British Isles, but those whose colouring can honestly be described as "brilliant" are few. Among these, the Goldfinch must always figure prominently, for in his case Nature has applied colours bright enough to match any competition. The scarlet patch about the forehead and throat, the white cheeks and golden-brown body, the rich yellow wing bars and black markings, give the Goldfinch the appearance of radiating colour and brilliance. The female is slightly less brightly dressed. Male and female are both about 13 cm in length.

The bird's fondness for orchards and gardens and, later in the year, when nesting is over, the field, where he goes to feed off thistle seeds, offers excellent opportunities of watching him in his natural setting.

Goldfinches are welcome visitors to any garden. They do no damage to buds or fruit, but thrive upon the many insect pests they find there as well as the seeds of thistle, dock, dandelion and other unwanted weeds. The bird sings a sweet note. Except for Scotland he is a familiar sight throughout these islands.

He may choose one of several nesting-sites. It may be in a hedge or garden shrub, or it may be in the branches of an odd fruit tree. He takes some pride in nest-building and fashions a neat, cosy home from wool, hair and grasses, which receive a lining of moss and feathers. In this comfortable recess up to five green-white eggs touched with red-brown tints are laid during May. Two families are reared.

Among many local names by which the Goldfinch is known are two apt ones – Thistle Finch and Seven-coloured Linnet.

THE BRAMBLING

THE BRAMBLING is a member of the finch family, although he is not a resident bird, coming here as a winter visitor. He usually arrives in the late autumn and leaves in the early spring. Bramblings often land in large numbers and make for the leaf-carpeted beech woods. On such occasions you may see small flocks of them rummaging industriously among the leaves and taking their fill of beechmast. When disturbed, they rise in a flurried body and disappear into the nearest cover.

During their winter stay the Bramblings often join the ranks of our resident finches, searching in the open fields for seeds and berries. In these islands the birds usually keep to the North and East.

The Brambling is a soberly-clad bird. Head, cheeks, neck, and back are blue-black; the rump is white. The throat and breast are fawn-red, and the belly is white. He has a length of six inches.

Of the bird's nesting-habits in his Northern home Howard Saunders writes: "As a rule the Brambling breeds at higher altitudes than those frequented by the Chaffinch; and its nest – usually placed where a branch meets the stem of a birch or fir tree, but sometimes in small juniper bushes – is bulkier, less compact and largely composed of birch-bark. Several pairs generally breed in company. The eggs, six to seven in number, laid late in May or early in June, are, as a rule, rather greener than those of the Chaffinch and have more defined markings."

The Brambling's song, the same authority tells us, "consists of several flute-like notes."

The bird is also known as the Mountain Finch.

THE LINNET

BUT FOR the unhappy practice of caging him for his song – a fate no wild bird deserves – the Linnet would be even less known than he already is. He is not a conspicuous bird but there should be no difficulty in finding him in his haunts. A gorse common or stretch of wild open heath-land is the country he prefers. Here he searches out the seed of linseed and hemp, and the insects and berries which form his food. These birds are usually to be found in colonies and on this account it is possible to watch more than one pair at a time.

The Linnet is one of few birds whose plumage changes colour during the year. But the coat by which he is best known is his smart spring one, when his crown and forehead are a crimson, his neck a smoky-brown, and his back a chestnut brown. A blurred white chin and throat and belly offset the crimson richness of the breast. The female is more quietly clad. The bird has a length of 14.5 cm.

When April comes in the paired birds look round for a nesting site. The dense furze bushes about their haunts are their most popular choice, although they will sometimes use a thorn hedge. The materials used are twigs, grass and moss, which receive a lining of hair. It is a most cosy structure. Up to six white, blue-tinged eggs, carrying markings of red-brown and purple-red, are laid. Two broods are usual.

Grey Linnet, Brown or Rose Linnet are familiar local names.

THE LESSER REDPOLL

TO THOSE people who like to observe and study the birds of the countryside, the Lesser Redpoll is an obliging little fellow who does not object to you getting a "close-up" of him. Neither is he averse to spending some time in gardens, where he sometimes presents the most convenient opportunities for watching his activities. The Lesser Redpoll is the smallest of the finch family.

The natural haunt of the bird is the woodland. His food in the summer is mainly of insects, in winter it is mainly of seeds. In winter, as do all the finches, the Lesser Redpolls move about in large flocks.

His song has the theme of the Linnet's but, while pleasing, lacks the Linnet's sweet quality. Except that certain areas of England are favoured for breeding, the Lesser Redpoll is to be met with almost everywhere in the British Isles.

The plumage of this engaging little bird is one of reds and browns. The outstanding note on top is the deep red patch of forehead and crown. The back is a warm brown. Below, a black throat enriches the rose-red breast. The female is more drab. The bird has a length of 11.5 cm.

The nesting-site of this bird varies. Hedges and bushes seem to be favoured, but trees such as alders and willows fringing streams or ponds are also used. The nest is a neat one made from twigs, moss and grass, the lining being of willow down. Up to six light olive-green eggs, carrying red-brown spots, are laid between May and June. Two families are usual.

A charming local name is Cherry Linnet.

THE SISKIN

A LTHOUGH a few pairs of these birds breed at times in the fir woods of Scotland and certain other areas of these islands, they are for the most part winter visitors who come here from Scandinavia and Russia. The Siskin wanders widely about the country and is often to be seen in the company of our finches during the winter. The seeds of the birch and alder are much favoured by Siskins and it is usually in the vicinity of these trees that he is to be found. Nevertheless he will also feed off insects as well as the seeds of various weeds and grasses. His songnotes have a pleasing quality.

The autumn coat of the Siskin lacks the richness of his spring suit which at that season is at its best. A black head-patch joins a back of green-tinged olive and yellow rump. Below, the black chin borders cheeks of a blurred green. Over the eye is a broad strip of yellow, the upper breast carrying the same colour. The hen bird is more soberly dressed. The Siskin has a length of just over 11.5 cm.

The bird nests fairly early in the spring and a favourite site is on a branch of a fir high up in the tree. The birch is also used, and occasionally, as Howard Saunders tells us, "gorse and other bushes" are nested in. Roots, twigs and moss are used in the making of the shell, which is lined with hair. Up to five off-white, blue-tinged eggs, with markings of red-brown, are laid. Two families are usually reared.

THE CROSSBILL

U NUSUAL or oddly-shaped bills are more common among our larger birds like the Curlew, Avocet and Spoonbill, but the colourful Crossbill can claim to be the owner of a beak that marks him out from our smaller birds. It is a bill of which the upper and lower mandibles cross over where they meet at the bottom, a tip jutting out each side like a pair of scissors partly open. His crossed bill is just the right tool for nipping out the seeds of fir cones, and for dealing with the insects, berries and fruit with which he varies his diet. Of the manner in which he tackles the cones R. M. Lockley writes: "Ripe and green cones are nipped off with the strong crossed bill and carried to a firm position on a branch or in dense greenery. Each one is held with the feet while the very efficient beak tears the scales asunder."

A few of these birds nest in the Southern Counties of England, but the main breeding haunts of the Crossbill in these islands are in the forests of Scotland. They keep mostly to the fir and pine tree areas.

The Crossbill is handsomely plumaged in an upper and lower mantle of rich deep crimson. The female is coloured green. The bird has a length of 16.5 cm.

Between February and March a nest is built. Usually it is sited in a pine or fir, sometimes low down but more generally high up. The frame is made from roots, twigs and grass and fitted with a warm lining of hair and wool. Up to five white, green-tinged, red-brown spotted eggs are laid.

THE HOUSE SPARROW

TO TOWNSPEOPLE, the House Sparrow is unquestionably the most familiar of all British birds. This gregarious little fellow, who seeks the society of man as eagerly as he does the company of his own kind, Is to be seen wherever there are buildings to give him shelter. There, in any convenient crevice, he will construct a sprawling nest of hay and straw to which he adds an untidy lining of feathers and any other soft material that may be available. House Sparrows raise at least two broods each year. The eggs usually number about five and vary considerably in colour and markings. A dingy-white background mottled with dark brown are the most common but markings varying in colour from chocolate to olive green are by no means rare.

All sorts of charges have been levelled against the House Sparrow. He is greedy and quarrelsome, he nips off the young shoots in the garden and he does no little damage to the buildings in which he makes his home. Yet our towns and cities would be poorer places without him. His perky self-assurance and his bold venturesome spirit reflect something of the characteristics of the British people. It is impossible not to feel some admiration and affection for him.

There is nothing particularly noteworthy in the House Sparrow's appearance. His colouring is one of sober brown merging into ash-grey and black on the breast and underside. Nevertheless the cock bird has the air of being well-groomed as he hops around in search of food; he, at least, seems well pleased with his costume.

The House Sparrow measures 15 cm in length.

THE TREE SPARROW

MOIST, rushy land in which the pollard willow thrives is a favourite haunt of the Tree Sparrow. He is not a very common bird, probably being as scarce as the House Sparrow is numerous, but he may be found in most parts of the British Isles, if not in great numbers.

Nine out of ten people would probably mistake him for his more common cousin, as in plumage and general appearance they are very much alike. The slight differences between them are noticeable in the rich brown head of the Tree Sparrow, and the black strip running into the white cheeks, both of which features are absent in the House Sparrow. The fact, too, that the Tree Sparrow is essentially a bird of the rural spaces should help in recognizing him. Both birds use a similar call-note, although it is said that the chirping of the Tree Sparrow has more melody to it. In the early part of the year the bird lives chiefly on insects of various kinds; but later, when seeds become available in the hedgerows, it finds a welcome variation to its diet.

The warmest note in the plumage of this bird is the chestnut-brown crown and neck. Below, it is chiefly a blurred white. He has a length of 14 cm.

The nesting sites of the Tree Sparrow are many but the one most used is a suitable hole in a pollard. Up to five grey-white eggs, with amber-brown markings, are laid during April in an untidy nest made from straw and hay and a lining of feathers and other oddments. At least two families are bred.

A local name for the bird is Mountain Sparrow.

THE CORN BUNTING

AS HIS name implies, the Corn Bunting is ever ready to take his fill from the green fields, but he also spends much time in pastures and open land, feeding on pests and harmful grubs which, during the breeding season, he feeds to the nestlings. This bird, which reminds me somewhat of a light-coloured Sparrow, may often be seen perched on a hedge-top or telegraph wire, whence he offers a good view of himself as he utters his few notes of song. In this he is a poor performer, for there is little quality in his singing.

Fondness for grain takes the Corn Bunting to the corn-yielding areas of the country. Here he may be encountered without much difficulty although he is not as numerous as his more colourful cousin, the Yellow Bunting. In the winter the Corn Bunting moves about in large colonies.

The Cirl and Yellow Buntings are more attractively plumaged than the Corn Bunting, whose topcoat has a general tone of a light warm brown; the undercoat is a shade or two paler, the breast carrying an area of spots. He has a length of 18 cm.

Any spot in a field which offers dense, concealing shelter, may be chosen for a nursery; there is usually a handy perch not far off. The bird shows little craftsmanship in the building of the nest, which is a straggling sort of structure made from straw, roots and coarse tangly grasses, with a lining of fine roots and hair. The four to five eggs laid late in May vary in colour; some have a ground tone of light yellow, others are a blurred purple white.

THE YELLOW BUNTING

TWO POINTS of interest about this bird are his more familiar name of Yellow Hammer and his reed-like song-notes which are often described as uttering the words "A little bit of bread and no cheese." This song is sometimes heard on a bright day in February, but during the summer months it is repeated again and again as the bird flits from twig to twig in the hedgerows.

The Yellow Bunting is a bird of the open countryside. During the early months of the year he satisfies his appetite from the varied insect-life he finds in the hedges and trees, but later, when the berries ripen and there is grain in the fields, he readily welcomes a change of diet. There are not many places in these islands where you may not stumble on these handsome little buntings – even in London they may occasionally be seen in gardens but shortly removed from the traffic's roar.

Wherever the Yellow Bunting perches, the yellow-golds of his mantle at once catch the eye. His bright yellow head, throat, breast and belly are favourably set off by a red-brown back, broken by markings of black. The breast has brown pencillings. He is 16.5 cm in length.

The nesting-site chosen by this bird is usually some well screened site close to the ground; sometimes a hedge or bush will be selected. Dead grasses form the framework of the nest, which is lined with hair. The four to five eggs laid early in May vary in colour; but the common ground tone is a purple-white. The markings of purple-brown bear a strong resemblance to a pen and ink scrawl and have consequently given the bird a local name of Scribbling Lark. Two or more families are bred.

THE CIRL BUNTING

THE CIRL BUNTING is another bird of the open countryside and arable lands. You will more often find him in the branches of a tree than the Yellow Bunting, whose general appearance he shares. His notes are similar too, and his feeding habits follow closely the fare favoured by his brighter coloured cousin. I have seen the Cirl Bunting more often in the counties of Devon and Somerset than elsewhere, but according to E. W. Hendy the bird is spreading to other parts of these islands. He visits, and at times nests in, gardens, and the chances of seeing him at close range are good. He hasn't quite the yellow brightness of the Hammer but his black throat makes a fine contrast and is a sure clue to his identity. He is an engaging little bird of quiet habits and cheery presence.

His plumage of broken yellows and olives is an attractive one. The olive crown and neck merge into a chestnut-brown back. A bright yellow strip runs over the eye. A light yellow band divides the black throat and splash of olive-green and blurred yellow breast. The rest of the underside is yellow. He has a length of 16.5 cm.

Nesting is sometimes started in late April, but May is the usual month. Somewhere in a low clump of furze or other bush is a favoured site, although occasionally a nest may be found actually on the ground. The shell is made from straw, roots and grass into which goes a lining of hair. Four, sometimes five, purple-blue, brown-black "scribbled" eggs are laid. At least two families are bred.

Black-throated Yellow Hammer is an aptly descriptive local name.

THE REED BUNTING

THE REED BUNTING makes his home by a stretch of water or sedgy marsh, and uses as a look-out perch the rushes or osiers which grow in the vicinity. From a slender rush-top he whistles his few notes, which have the bunting theme but have perhaps more melody. Unlike many birds haunting marshland the Reed Bunting does not flit off at first sight of an intruder. He is altogether bolder and gives the bird-lover a fair chance of watching his movements. As in the case of the other buntings, his diet during the early months of the year is mainly of insects; later seeds and grain become his staple food. In those areas of the British Isles which provide the sort of surroundings he favours, the Reed Bunting is by no means a rare bird.

More soberly clad than his cousins, the Reed Bunting is no less attractive. He is smartest in his spring suit. Head, throat and breast of a rich black are divided by a band of white which circles the neck. The back is a pleasing red-brown, the belly is white. The female is more quietly attired. The bird has a length of 15 cm.

The Reed Bunting makes use of several nesting-sites. He likes them about his haunt and near water. Rushes are often used, or the tall grasses of a bank. Now and again low bush is chosen. Grass, moss and reed stems form the frame, hair and reed flowers the lining. The usual colouring of the four to five eggs laid during May is purple-grey with markings of purple-brown. At least two families are reared.

The bird is widely known as the Reed Sparrow.

THE SNOW BUNTING

ALTHOUGH the natural breeding grounds of the Snow Bunting are on the fringes of the Arctic Circle a few of these birds nest with us, chiefly in the mountainous parts of Scotland and the Shetland Isles. A number of them arrive here as winter visitors. On their arrival towards the end of October they form into flocks, some of which as R. M. Lockley tells us, may usually be seen "on the inner salt marshes of the Thames and regularly farther out along the Essex shore."

At this time of the year they are a familiar sight about the foreshore of our coastline. In spring and summer these birds live on insects; later in the year seeds are taken. The bird possesses a few warbling notes which he sings during nesting-time.

Like the Linnet the Snow Bunting changes his coat during the year; and although he lacks the warmer colours of many of our birds, his nearly all-white plumage gives him an elegant appearance. Except for a black back and a few patches of the same colour, the spring mantle of this bird is largely white. He has a length of 17 cm.

Gaunt rocks and outcrops provide the Snow Bunting with a nesting-site very difficult to discern. Having selected a concealed crevice, the paired birds furnish it with dry grasses, roots and moss, which they weave into the outer shell. This is lined with deer's hair and feathers. The eggs of which up to six are laid during May, vary in their base colour, some being cream-tinged, others a light blue; they are commonly marked in red-brown.

A local name expressing the beauty of this bird is Snow-flake.

THE STARLING

THERE are few places in the British Isles where the Starling may not be seen in abundant numbers. He is certainly not shy and he takes no pains to conceal himself from man. His comical waddle about the lawns of our gardens is a familiar sight and his thin, plaintive whistle is one of the bird-sounds that never seem to cease. The Starling is a great mimic, often singing the songs of other birds with astonishing accuracy, although he can produce a tuneful melody on his own account.

The Starling has the unfortunate habit of nesting in the eaves of houses and in open drain-pipes, a practice not encouraged by the majority of householders. Nor does pilfering of fruit and small shoots endear him to gardeners; although, to offset this, he wreaks great destruction among garden pests and harmful grubs.

His spring plumage is dark but colourful. Its general tones are a metallic purple-green. The bird's one strong colour-note is his long yellow bill. He has a length of 21.5 cm.

In his rural haunts the Starling's nest is usually constructed deep down in a tree-hole, but any site that takes his fancy may be as readily used. The materials are straw and moss with feathers for a lining. The nest is as untidy as the Sparrow's. The four to six eggs laid early in April, sometimes at the end of March, are a delicate pale blue. More than one brood is reared.

Immense flocks of these birds roost together at night during the winter on London's tall buildings.

THE CARRION CROW

ALMOST every type of country from woodland to seashore is attractive to the Carrion Crow; sometimes he will even settle down in the very heart of human habitations provided that trees and a stretch of open land are not too far off.

Few British birds are more wary and resourceful, few are more able to meet the everyday dangers of wild life.

The Carrion Crow is a confirmed robber of other bird's eggs and nestlings, ranking in this respect with those other expert nest thieves, the Jay and Magpie. He will strike down birds and small animals too weak or too scared to defend themselves, or will enjoy a meal of noisome carrion such as other creatures would not even approach. His is not a pleasant character even though he may account for the destruction of quantities of vermin.

The Carrion Crow is rare in Ireland and avoids the Northern parts of Scotland. Elsewhere, he breeds freely throughout these islands, although he is more plentifully found in some areas than in others.

The rich, silky black plumage of this bird, broken by tints of purple and green, is too familiar to need further description. He has a length of about 40-50 cm.

Nest-building is begun about the second week in April, the nest usually being placed in the branches of a tall tree. A cliff-face or rocky ledge near the ground is also used at times. The framework is a large structure of sticks and twigs plastered with mud or clay. The lining is generally of wool, hair and feathers. Up to five light-green, blue-tinged eggs, with markings of brown, are laid. It is thought that the Carrion Crow pairs for life.

THE ROOK

ALTHOUGH the Rook is by nature a bird of the open country he is often quite content to live on the fringe of towns and cities. Where there are elms, you may expect to find colonies, both large and small, of these birds. At a little distance it is possible to mistake a Rook for a Crow, but the error can be quickly determined by a sight of the Rook's bald face compared with the black, feathered face of the Crow.

His croak is deeper than the Crow's. And he usually caws four or more times to the Crow's normal three. The Rook is slightly smaller than the Crow.

It can be said against the Rook that he damages growing crops and sometimes may swoop up a pheasant chick or nestling partridge; but the Rook is also a great destroyer of the grubs and insects turned up by the plough and it is universally conceded that he is the friend rather than the enemy of the farmer. The bird is well spread about the British Isles.

Except for the grey-white face and yellowish bill the plumage is a rich silky black shot with a violet-blue tinge. He has a length of just under 48 cm.

The bulky nest of the Rook must be familiar to most people. The large numbers of nests which comprise many rookeries are used year after year by the same birds. Each year additions and repairs are made to the old structures so that in some cases the nests assume very considerable proportions. The frame is made from sticks and twigs kept together with a plastering of mud or clay and lined with straw and grasses. Up to five light blue-green eggs with markings of brown-green are laid during March.

THE JACKDAW

O F ALL wild birds, the Jackdaw responds most readily to the advances of man. With but slight encouragement he quickly overcomes his natural suspicion and fear and learns to take titbits of food from the hand. He is a great hoarder and he cannot resist bright and shining objects. The combination of these two instincts has many times produced the most remarkable treasure trove which the Daw has diligently collected and concealed.

Although the Jackdaw will readily consume fruit and garden produce, or pilfer eggs from game preserves, he is mainly an insect-eater, devouring during the course of the year large quantities of harmful insects of various kinds. He is the bird you will sometimes see on the back of a sheep helping to rid the animal of the parasites which live in its wool. Daws, like the Rooks, often live together in large colonies. He is no stranger anywhere in these islands, although he is more numerous in England and Wales.

The Jackdaw is smaller than the Rook or Crow – being about 36 cm in length – he is not unlike the two larger birds in appearance. Like theirs his plumage is black, but has an area of grey over the back of the neck which marks him out quite distinctly from the others.

The Daw is fond of setting up his home in a church tower or a stone ruin, but trees, chimneys and even rabbit burrows are equally acceptable. The large, bulky nest is put together with sticks and straws and is lined chiefly with wool. Up to six light blue-green eggs, with markings of ash, dark brown or black, are laid in the latter part of April.

THE MAGPIE

A COMMON sight in the countryside is the smart and attractive Magpie. But he's a bird with a bad name and, according to superstition, of ill-omen. He is an inveterate robber of other birds' nests, taking either eggs or nestlings, and he does not hesitate to plunder wherever food to his taste is available. Nevertheless, some part of his diet is made up of small vermin and farmland pests so that his character is not without its redeeming features. The Magpies' haunts are usually well-wooded and in such areas throughout the British Isles he is to be found without difficulty. His constant chatter is a very familiar country sound.

The plumage of this bird is most attractive, especially when, as often happens, his long tail and wings are fully spread at the moment of touching ground. The black parts of the Magpie – head, neck, back and breast – which bear shadings of violet and green have, like the rest of his feathers, a satiny richness. The shoulders stand out in clear white patches; the belly is also white. The female is not quite as colourful. The bird has a length of 46 cm.

Robber though he is of other birds' nests the Magpie takes good care to protect his own. A tall hedge or other green clump may sometimes be used for nesting in, but the more usual site is high up in the branches of a giant tree. It is made in the form of a dome from thorn sticks which are plastered together with mud or clay. Into this goes a lining of grasses and roots. The entrance is at the side. This massive construction is a fine, weatherproof, workmanlike job to which the birds often return the following year. Up to eight, sometimes more, light blue-green, brown-spotted eggs are laid during April.

THE JAY

THE JAY, like the Crow and Magpie, feeds readily on eggs and fledglings stolen from other birds' nests. On this account, his presence is far from welcome in country where game is preserved and he is often shot on sight. But despite the number of these birds shot each year by farmers and gamekeepers, his wary, resourceful nature enables him to survive all onslaughts, and in some areas where the cover is good even to increase his numbers.

The Jay is a native of the woodlands, but he likes to roam about the countryside. Sometimes he will even make his headquarters in a garden, where he will wreak havoc among the peas and fruits, and scold every intruder in his domain with angry screech-notes.

The Jay's spring suit is very smart. Crowning his head is an imposing black and white crest; his neck and back are a fawny-red enlivened by a splash of white on the rump. The tail is black. A characteristic colour-note is the light blue patch on the wing coverts, which is barred with blacks and whites. The chin and most of the under-mantle is a light buff, warmer on the sides. The bird has a length of about 36 cm.

The nest, usually sited fairly high up in some tree in a dense part of the wood, is made chiefly from twigs and has a lining of grasses and soft roots. Up to six, sometimes more, dull-green, brown-marked eggs are laid during April and May.

This dapper bird of the woodlands is well represented in the timbered areas of the British Isles.

THE KESTREL

WHENEVER I see this handsome hawk quartering a patch of country in search of prey, it occurs to me that his less familiar name of Windhover is infinitely more apt and descriptive than that by which he is commonly called. His manner of hanging almost motionless in the air as his all-seeing eyes follow the course of a rat or rabbit below is a familiar sight in most parts of these islands. The sudden swoop from aloft as he drops like a stone invariably marks the end of some small creature, usually vermin, which the Kestrel had marked out for his quarry. Although he prefers to feed on rats, mice and beetles, he will on occasion take small birds. I recall seeing a Kestrel, one cold afternoon in February, pounce with perfect precision upon an unsuspecting Sparrow as it hopped about the rime-covered grass of my lawn.

By nature the Kestrel is a bird of the woodlands but he will readily hunt in a suburban area broken by roads and houses. I have seen a pair of these hawks skim no more than a few feet above a passing omnibus when making for a nearby field.

The upper mantle of the Kestrel is one of blue-greys and a rich light chestnut; the lower is chiefly of buff with markings of black. The bird has a length of 36 cm.

The Kestrel is little interested in nest-building. The disused nest of some other bird, usually that of a Crow or Rook, is used in which to lay, during April, the four to six red-brown eggs, mottled in a darker shade of the same colour.

A local name is Mouse Falcon.

THE SPARROW HAWK

THE HAUNT of the Sparrow Hawk is woodland surrounded by open country. He is a clever hunter who makes good use of every tree and hedge in his path to effect surprise. Every movement of this graceful bird suggests striking power and merciless precision. His method is to skim low towards a field in which birds are feeding, and suddenly to appear from behind a rick or through a gate. Usually he takes his prey on the wing. As an alternative method he will conceal himself in the branches of a tree whence he will make his death-dealing sallies with incredible speed. He preys chiefly on birds: the Sparrow, Lark, Blackbird, Thrush and Pigeon, but he will sometimes take young hares, rats and mice. Large insects are also eaten.

The boldness and determination of the Sparrow Hawk is such that he will follow his prey no matter into what danger he may be led. There have been many cases recorded in which both pursued and pursuer met their ends by crashing into netting, telephone wires or glass windows. The bird is well spread throughout the British Isles.

The Sparrow Hawk's mantle is an attractive one of slate-blue with markings of red-brown on a warm buff below. The female is the larger bird. The cock bird has a length of 30 cm.

Trees are the customary nesting-places, and quite often the deserted nest of a Crow or other large bird will be taken over. The materials used are sticks for the frame and twigs for the lining. Up to six light blue-white eggs with red-brown markings are laid during May.

A local name is Blue Hawk.

THE TAWNY OWL

THE LONG-DRAWN, plaintive hoot of the largest of our resident owls is more widely known to the public than the bird himself. The Tawny Owl, living though he often does in parks and woodlands close to human dwellings, does not readily show himself, and then usually only in the twilight or nightfall. For it is as darkness falls that he embarks on His hunting expeditions.

The fields with their teeming wild life are the natural larder of the Tawny Owl, and he takes great toll from them, especially when there are owlets to be fed. Young hares and rabbits, mice and moles, are caught with unerring skill during the dark hours of the night. Beetles and other small creatures are also taken.

Except for some parts of Scotland, where he is very scarce, the Tawny Owl is fairly well dispersed throughout the wooded areas of the British Isles.

His general colour, as his name suggests, is a rich tawny, marked and mottled in darker shades of the same colour. He has a length of 40 cm.

A tree-hole is the most likely nesting-place of the Tawny Owl, although he will occasionally take over the deserted nest of a Magpie, Rook or Crow, or even the drey of a squirrel. The bones and other indigestible portions of his diet which he has regurgitated form the lining of the nesting-chamber, though sometimes a feather or two will be used. Up to seven glossy white eggs are laid during March.

Brown Owl, Wood Owl, and Ivy Owl are a few of the local names the bird has been given.

THE BARN OWL

A T ONE time farmers did all they could to keep the Barn Owl from their farms because it was thought that these birds took a heavy toll of young chicks from the hen-yards and game preserves. This belief has been effectively disproved and the Barn Owl is now welcomed as a tireless and invaluable destroyer of rats, mice and all the other vermin which flourish in ricks and corn-stacks. Although the name of this bird suggests the farmstead and countryside, Barn Owls are by no means rare in towns and cities, and many an old church surrounded by the habitations of man gives shelter and a nursery to these birds.

I can well recall a pair of Barn Owls regularly taking up their perch in the branches of a tall tree in a London garden of my acquaintance. As dusk drew in their piercing screech told us that the grim all-night hunt had begun.

The Barn Owl is an attractive bird of some 36 cm with a white face, warm buff head and neck and under-mantle chiefly of white.

The weather-beaten rafters of some old barn, steeple or hollow tree are places the Barn Owl will readily choose for a nesting-site. He makes little or no attempt to line it. Up to eight blurred white eggs, sometimes laid in pairs, are in their nest by the end of April. It is no unusual thing to see unhatched eggs and nestlings together.

Screech Owl is a popular name for this bird.

THE LONG-EARED OWL

THIS HANDSOME bird with yellow eyes and long ear tufts is very much an owl of the forest. Normally he will be found only in the depths of a green-laced thicket in the heart of the country. He is a very cautious and suspicious bird where man is concerned, and the opportunity to see him usually comes only as a result of patient planning and waiting. Nevertheless, good fortune sometimes provides a chance encounter with him during the day as he dozes peacefully in a tree-cleft. At least, that's what he appears to be doing. More often the wary bird is far from asleep, and when he thinks you've come as close to him as he cares about, he will fly off into the dense screen of foliage surrounding him and you will see him no more.

The Long-eared Owl, like our other owls, lives on rats, mice, small birds and similar fare. He is to be found in most wooded parts of the British Isles.

Many mottlings of brown and grey adorn the plumage of the Long-eared Owl, whose upper coat is mainly a buff colour. The face, too, is of this colour. The under-mantle is a buff-brown. He has a length of 38 cm.

Nest-building has little interest for him. One given up by the Wood Pigeon, Magpie, Crow or Rook will be taken over. Sometimes a few twigs or a little hair is used as a lining. Nesting is early. Up to five, sometimes six, white eggs are laid during March.

Compared with the Barn and Tawny Owls, whose hoots are seemingly ceaseless, the Long-eared Owl is a silent bird. He utters only a short bark-like note.

THE SHORT-EARED OWL

WOODLANDS have little if any attraction for the Short-eared Owl, whose haunt is the marsh and moor. In these bleak and lonely wastes he feeds lavishly on field mice, rats, birds and game fowl. In the autumn our native Short-eared Owls are joined by large numbers from abroad, who are often to be seen in the cornfields after harvest and among the turnips. Here they destroy voles and mice in great quantities, and much valuable work has been done by these birds in the past when hordes of field mice seriously threatened the crops of many farms.

Scotland rather than England is the home of the Short-eared Owl, where he is fairly numerous as a breeder. In England only a few of these owls nest. It is the visiting birds who spread themselves about England.

The Short-eared Owl, although chiefly a nocturnal bird, may occasionally be seen quartering the fields by day.

The plumage of this bird is well streaked and marked in blacks and browns, but the general tones of his mantle above are a light buff; the undercoat has a warmer tone of the same colour. The face is off-white. He has a length of 36.5 cm.

In marshland the nest is usually sited in a patch of sedge; on moorland, in the heather. Up to seven white eggs are laid during April and May.

Marsh Owl is another name for this bird, but because the migrants arrive at approximately the same time as the Woodcock he is also known as the Woodcock Owl.

THE LITTLE OWL

THE LITTLE OWL may quite often be seen by day. On occasions he will perch on a telegraph pole or some equally exposed position boldly offering an excellent view of himself. Nevertheless, the Little Owl is nocturnal by nature, hunting chiefly at night. There are many theories why this owl should be so much more in evidence during daylight hours than others of his kind. So far, there has been no satisfactory explanation although some of the speculations are as interesting as they are ingenious. His favourite haunt is the woodland.

The Little Owl is not strictly a native of the British Isles as are the Barn or Tawny Owls. He was introduced into England many years ago, since when he has not only greatly increased and become very much a British bird, but has spread himself far afield. He is, however, seen less in the North. His larder is the fields and trees in which he finds many kinds of insects as well as his usual fare of rats, mice and small birds.

The general tones of his plumage carry varied markings of grey-brown above and blurred white below. He has a length of just under 23 cm. He is the smallest of our resident owls.

The Little Owl shares with the rest of his tribe a disinclination to build his own nest. He makes use of any handy place he finds about the countryside – hollow tree, barn, wall or old nest. Up to five white eggs are laid during April and May.

THE WOOD PIGEON

THE SOFT cooing note of this bird, who comes from the woodlands but whose food is the produce and fruit he can pick up from field, garden and orchard, is a familiar sound in all country districts. A circle of white feathers about his neck has given him an alternative name of Ring Dove and is a quick aid in picking him out from his three cousins, the Stock, Turtle and Rock Doves.

The bird is no stranger to most parts of the British Isles and, on account of his depredations, is far from liked by the farmer and orchard owner. Yet purely as a wild bird he is an attractive creature about the countryside. He is a town dweller too, but even in towns he will cling to his natural preference for trees as opposed to buildings in which to establish his nest. Nor does he take readily to street scavenging, preferring to go to the parks and gardens for his daily food.

Blue-greys and slate-greys are the basic tones of the Wood Pigeon's upper plumage. The lower part is of a pleasing purple-wine on the breast, the belly being lighter. The bird has a length of 42.5 cm.

Two glossy white eggs are laid during March in a flimsy structure of twigs high up in a tree, hedge or bush. The nestlings take their food from the pulp contained in the crops of the parent birds. At least two families are reared and sometimes a third quite late in the year. The male bird does part of the sitting.

THE STOCK DOVE

THE STOCK DOVE is the second of the four attractive pigeons which breed here. Like his cousins he is fond of grain and whatever else he can carry off from the fields and gardens about his haunt, including the seeds of various weeds. He is a smaller bird than the Wood Pigeon and much shyer, flitting off with a flapping of wings the moment he detects a threat to his safety.

Where there is an abundance of old trees the Stock Dove will readily settle, and in most timbered areas of these islands he is a fairly familiar figure. In spite of this he is much less common than the Wood Pigeon. He has a low crooning note.

The chief colour-motif in the plumage of the Stock Dove is his wine-red breast, offset by a mingling of blue-greys. The neck carries a glossy touch of green and purple. The female is a smaller bird and is more quietly dressed. The male has a length of just under 36 cm.

For the most part the Stock Dove uses a hole in a tree in which to nest, but in the neighbourhood of the coast he often rears his family in a sand burrow. Other nesting-sites are on old beams of barns or in the disused nests of other birds. A first clutch of two white eggs is laid during April.

Blue-backed Dove is another name by which this bird is known in rural districts.

THE TURTLE DOVE

THE TURTLE DOVE comes each year to the British Isles from Africa, arriving towards the end of April or early in May. He is usually off again during September, sometimes later. He keeps for the most part to the Southern areas of England.

His soft, cooing note is a familiar sound in woodland areas and blends well with the quiet of the countryside. He is the smallest of our doves.

His diet is largely of grain taken from the fields and of seeds found in the hedgerow. In common with the other doves, the Turtle Dove drinks much water. This point is brought out by John Kearton, who writes: "All our Doves drink great quantities of water, particularly during hot weather, and have a habit of thrusting their bills deep into a pool and sucking the liquid up after the manner of a cow or horse."

The Turtle Dove's plumage is more variedly tinted than that of his cousins'. Most noticeable is the small area of black and white on each side of the neck. The blue-grey of the head and neck joins a rich brown back. The throat and breast carry a light wine tint. The belly is white. The bird has a length of 29 cm.

The nesting-site is either a bush or a tree, and the nest is the familiar loose structure of twigs. Two white, cream-tinged eggs are laid between May and June.

TURTLE DOVE

IN ARCADIA

A series of beautifully illustrated books inspired by the many faces of the British countryside.

OTHER TITLES IN THIS SERIES

In the Heart of the Country • H.E. Bates
978-1-906509-83-5

The genius of H.E. Bates and C.F. Tunncliffe combine to show the magnificence of winter blizzards; the sudden sweet arrival of spring blossom; the heavy scent of an August garden; or the bronze glow of autumn light. Its pages are full of sharp observations which reveal the loveliness of everyday sights and fleeting moments, from the charm of butterflies and their names to the behaviour of animals and birds, the joys of gardening and the character of the people and their landscape.

The Happy Countryman • H.E. Bates
978-1-906509-82-8

Inspired by the gentle beauty of the English landscape, the celebrated writer H.E. Bates and the much loved wildlife artist C.F. Tunnicliffe produced an enchanting tribute to country life. With the deft, sure eye of master craftsmen, they portray the mellow stone of country towns, spray swept seaside promenades, strolls among sand dunes, Mr Pimpkins the jobbing gardener, roach fishing at dawn, the art of pear growing, and much more to make a book that is lasting pleasure. Above all, *The Happy Countryman* was H.E. Bates statement of his own ideals about the countryside and his hopes and fears for its future.

English Country Houses • Vita Sackville-West
978-1-910065-11-2

This book offers a brief history of the English country house from the Middle Ages to the 20th century, and of the people who built and lived in them – from common squires to kings and queens. Written during the Blitz by one of England's most celebrated writers, this text was undoubtedly a morale booster for a British people laid siege to during a time of war, a time when entire cities were being destroyed. *English Country Houses* demonstrates a yearning for the safety supplied by the buildings Vita Sackville-West describes.